LIVING
the Locavore
LIFESTYLE

Hunting, Fishing, Gathering Wild Fruit and Nuts,
Growing a Garden, and Raising Chickens toward
a More Sustainable and Healthy Way of Living

Bruce and Elaine Ingram

Secant Publishing, LLC
P.O. Box 79
Salisbury MD 21803

First Edition 2016

Paperback: 978-1-944962-03-6
Ebook (epub):   978-1-944962-04-3
Ebook (mobi):   978-1-944962-05-0
Library of Congress Control Number: 2016933079

Grateful acknowledgment is made to the following publications in which portions of this book were first published:

Several recipes for venison in Chapter 2 originally appeared in *Whitetail Times*, a publication of the Virginia Deer Hunters Association, and *Quality Whitetails*, a publication of the Quality Deer Management Association.

Several recipes for turkey meat in Chapter 4 originally appeared in *Turkey Country*, a publication of the National Wild Turkey Federation.

The recipe for sourdough bread in Chapter 4 is used with the permission of author Soc Clay.

Chapter 5, "Getting Started on Squirrel Hunting," appeared in slightly different form in *Turkey Country*, a publication of the National Wild Turkey Federation.

Chapter 16, "Wild Black Walnuts," appeared in slightly different form in *Turkey Country*, a publication of the National Wild Turkey Federation.

Portions of Chapter 23 originally appeared in *Grit* magazine.

Chapters 24 and 25, "Protecting Your Flock" and "The Heritage Chicken Option," appeared in the magazine *Back Home*.

"A Letter to my Grandson Sam" originally appeared in *Outdoor America*, a publication of the Izaak Walton League of America.

"The Fascination Began at Five" originally appeared in *Wildlife in North Carolina*.

"The Day I Became a Deer Hunter," "Hunting the Living Meat," and "It's My Dirt" appeared first in *Quality Whitetails*, a publication of the Quality Deer Management Association.

"She Still Can't Cast" originally appeared in *American Angler*.

Publisher's Note
The publisher is not responsible for the ingestion of any edibles discussed in this book. Each individual has different tolerances and allergies, and moreover, some wild plants and fungi can be universally toxic. Readers should seek the guidance of an expert in identifying and approving any unknown or unfamiliar edible substance before consumption.

Table of Contents

Preface

My wife Elaine and I were born in the 1950s, grew up in the suburbs of towns in Southwest Virginia where we came of age in the 1960s, and graduated from college, becoming school teachers, in the 1970s. Nothing in our respective backgrounds would predict that one day almost all of the red meat that we consume would come from wild game I kill; that most of our desserts, jams, jellies, and preserves would come from wild fruits and nuts we gather; that we would try to support local farmers whenever possible with the foodstuffs we purchase; or that we would become backyard chicken enthusiasts. Or even, for that matter, that we would become wild game food columnists for two publications.

But we did become devoted locavores—and so can you. The term *'locavore'* combines the word *local* with the Latin root for *devour* (think *carnivore* or *herbivore*). As locavores, we hunt, fish, forage, and grow as much of our diet as we can within short walking distance of our homestead—which is located on 38 acres of largely undeveloped land in Botetourt County, Virginia. I am fortunate to be able to hunt and fish behind our house, as well as on other properties nearby. Elaine and I annually gather over ten gallons of wild fruits and berries, delight in gathering various nuts in season, and raise a vegetable garden, fruit trees, and chickens in our backyard.

But owning rural land is not a prerequisite for leading a locavore-like lifestyle. Anyone with a backyard can raise a small garden, fruit trees, and a few chickens. Anyone with local farmers' markets—and thousands exist across the United States—can support the entrepreneurs who sell their produce there. Almost anyone who wants to fish can find lakes, streams, or ponds nearby. And anyone with a bucket can find places to gather nature's bounty.

It's true that hunting is generally a pastime where one needs a mentor to help him or her begin. But groups exist that specialize in helping novices learn to hunt. I didn't grow up in a family that hunted or fished, yet I became an outdoor writer who has written over 2,200 magazine articles and six books on the outdoors.

In the book that follows, the sections on hunting, fishing and gathering, and the essays at the end were written by Bruce. Elaine is responsible for the wonderful recipes that we both enjoy. Our life and lessons on living the locavore lifestyle have been shared by both of us and our family. We hope this slender volume can start you, too, on your way to becoming a locavore.

Introduction

Two of the questions I often receive from people who are thinking about becoming locavores are how much it will cost, and how much it will save. No universal answer exists for those questions. So much depends on the individual. Here's how I answer.

About 40 years ago, I decided to stop eating pork; about 25 years ago, I gave up beef; and about a dozen years ago, Elaine and I stopped buying poultry meat, except from animals that had been raised so as to produce organic meat. As I write this, the deer seasons have just ended in Virginia and West Virginia where I do most of my hunting (we live near the border between the two states and own land in both Virginias). I killed a total of eleven deer (Virginia offers bonus tags that allow for extra antlerless deer to be killed), and of those eleven, Elaine and I butchered four. Our butcher charged us a total of $435 to process the other whitetails; usually, the butcher charges $60 to $65 per deer depending on size. I also killed four turkeys during the calendar year.

I have no idea what the cost of pork, beef, or non-organic poultry is and have no reason to find out as it doesn't concern me. I also want to emphasize that there's nothing wrong or un-locavorish about buying locally raised, grass-fed (also called pastured) pork and beef products. Our daughter Sarah and her husband David often buy a side of beef that came from a cow that spent its life in a pasture. One of my best friends, Paul Hinlicky, raises pastured pigs to sell. In both cases, this meat is healthy to eat and people who purchase it are wisely supporting local farmers whom we should support in order to keep Rural American rural.

What I do think people should strive to do, as much as possible, is purchase more meat, vegetables, fruits, and other foodstuffs that have been produced near their homes and raised in a healthy, humane way. Animals raised in small, metal boxes, animals that have been injected with growth hormones, arsenic, and antibiotics (even when they were not ill), and animals shipped hundreds or even thousands of miles are animals whose meat people may want to reconsider eating.

Annually, I kill a lot of deer and, hopefully, my limits of turkeys in the two Virginias, so that Elaine and I can be as self-sufficient and self-reliant as possible. I don't do so to save money, although I am guessing that we do. Can two American adults fulfill almost all of their protein needs for the year by spending $435?

In the summer, Elaine and I also gather ten or eleven gallons of wild berries. Come fall, we gather persimmons, pawpaws, grapes, black walnuts, and hickory nuts. We also grow apples, cherries, and crabapples in our backyard and vegetables in our garden, and raise chickens. We shop at a local supermarket for many of our vegetables because we can't grow enough in the summer to supply our year-long needs. Whenever possible, we go to farmer's markets to buy locally grown foodstuffs. Again, I don't know what the cost of a store-bought frozen pie or a cake is, and I don't care.

The reasons I hunt for food and the reasons we gather wild fruits and nuts, tend a garden and fruit trees, and raise chickens really have nothing to do with how much money we save. It's because being a locavore makes sense on so many levels. Hunting, fishing, gathering, growing, and raising chickens is great mentally and physically for any individual, couple, or family with children. I am 64 years old and am filled with energy and love life. Even though I am three years past retirement as a public school teacher, I don't want to retire; I love going to work every day and helping young people learn.

While out hunting, fishing, and gathering, I love to birdwatch, identify trees and wildlife, and be alone with my thoughts. The benefits of living this type of lifestyle cannot be quantified, but I do think it is a big part of the reason why I feel great mentally and physically, am rarely sick, and have a joy for life.

Here's another example of why I live the way I do. Recently, a young man half my age asked me to take him turkey hunting one morning. On his way to my house, he stopped at a fast food place, he said, and ate some sort of greasy, fried concoction. To reach where the turkeys would be roosting, we had to walk up a hill through a cow pasture, then ascend a mountain. The young man became winded walking up the hill, for goodness sakes. By the time we arrived at the foot of the mountain, he was truly exhausted and he told me he was afraid he would have a heart attack. For breakfast that morning, I had eaten, as usual, organically grown oatmeal with numerous kinds of fruits. I had not yet worked up a sweat and was still breathing normally when we arrived at the foot of the mountain. I have climbed that mountain many times and enjoy doing so. There is a huge difference between how I feel and how that young man does, and a monetary value cannot be put on that difference.

Laura Pole, who operates Eating for a Lifetime in Hardy, Virginia, is one of the most knowledgeable people I know on the topic of healthy eating. She says that a whole food diet with the addition of healthy animal foods such as wild game, pasture-raised livestock, and eggs from pastured chickens is the preferred diet that people should strive to follow. Venison, for example, is higher in many types of vitamins and minerals and lower in bad cholesterol than the meat from factory-farmed animals. Pole adds that grapes with their resveratrol, wild berries with their Vitamin C, flavonoids and anti-oxidants, and wild black walnuts (Omega 3s and 6s and Vitamins B6 and E) are also essential for good health.

As you read this book, I hope you will be encouraged to become more of a locavore. As someone who doesn't know the cost of many store items, I can't promise that you will save money. You will have to buy some things; for example, we had to buy a freezer for all our wild game bounty, and a second refrigerator to store the fruits and nuts we gather or buy locally, plus the 25-pound bags of organic oatmeal we purchase. I also have a feeling that the more you practice the locavore lifestyle, the more you will enjoy the natural world, enjoy the benefits of the exercise you are experiencing, and feel better physically and mentally. I don't think these things can have a price tag put on them.

1. Hunting and Eating Wild Game

As noted in the Preface, I do not come from a family that fished or hunted or, indeed, participated in outdoor recreation at all. My parents were children of the Great Depression, and their hardscrabble upbringing in the rural South left little time for pursuits that were regarded as frivolous. As a child, I often asked my father to take me hunting or fishing, but he never did, having no experience or interest with either, and working two full-time jobs himself.

At the age of 33, I went hunting for the first time in the fall of 1985 when a friend took me afield for squirrels. The year before, Elaine and I had bought our first rural property, a 30-acre tract in the Johns Creek Valley of Craig County, Virginia. So my buddy, who was an experienced squirrel hunter, and I drove there for my initial outing.

After we debarked from the car, my friend said we were going to still hunt down the access road entering the land. Still hunting is a tactic where an individual takes a few, slow steps at a time, then stops to look for movement on the ground, or in the case of squirrels, often in the trees. This gambit is extremely effective and it forces the individual to learn how to visualize the environment as a place alive with wildlife.

We walked about 50 yards when my mentor spotted hickory nut shells falling to the ground. My inexperienced eyes finally viewed the same thing. Then my friend told me to follow the falling shells upward to their source. Hickory nuts are a favorite food of gray and fox squirrels. A while later, I finally espied the gray squirrel making the commotion, so it was time for the next instructions. "Wait," my friend said, "until the squirrel is sitting still on a limb and eating a nut. Then raise the shotgun, put the bead on the squirrel's head, take a deep breath, and shoot."

I did as told and when the squirrel tumbled to the ground, I was convinced that a near miracle had happened. I don't remember how Elaine prepared that bushytail, but I do recall the sense of pride that I had bringing it to her. I likewise recall that no squirrel has ever tasted as good as that one—consuming something that one has brought home to the family instills a feeling of accomplishment that I still experience today, no matter whether it is wild game, fish, berries, or nuts.

Over the three-plus decades since, my wife has joyfully fixed all manners of creatures I have brought home… except for one. I once had friend Jay Honse offer to give me a snapping turtle he had caught in his pond. Snapping turtles are renowned for their tasty soups and their multiple kinds of meat that can be prepared any number of ways.

However, Elaine said under no circumstances was a snapper entering her house, no matter whether it was inside a shell or perfectly cleaned. Alas, unfortunately, this book will contain no snapping turtle recipes, per order of my wife. Here's how to start hunting other big and small game animals.

Still hunting is a very effective way to hunt many big and small game animals.

1. Getting Started on Deer Hunting

The whitetail deer is the most popular big game animal in America and certainly a fascinating quarry to pursue.

To begin to hunt for deer or any wild game, a first step adults and youth can take is to enroll in a hunter safety class. Some states offer these courses online, others require that individuals attend in person. Regardless, these classes offer a wealth of valuable information, especially about gun safety, hunter ethics, and the animals themselves. Nothing I can write here can in any way replace the crucial information gained from these classes.

Another step novices can take is to purchase an apprentice license from their state game departments or division of natural resources. Virginia's Sherry Crumley, former board chairman of the Virginia Department of Game and Inland Fisheries (VDGIF) and current board member for the National

Wild Turkey Federation (NWTF), helped initiate the Old Dominion's first apprentice license.

"People who buy apprentice licenses can have a veteran hunter show them the basics of hunting and mentor them," says Sherry. "Another benefit of apprentice licenses is that they are cheaper than regular licenses, so novices can try out hunting, so to speak."

Sherry is also an active advocate of more girls and women taking up the pastime of hunting.

"Women are very much a part of the move to the locavore lifestyle," she says. "They are used to doing the food shopping and what could be more local than meat from the animal you kill in the county where you live."

One of the aspects concerning hunting that Sherry and I have in common is that we both began hunting as adults, in her case when she was 39. Her husband Jim, famous as the inventor of modern day camouflage with his Trebark brand, offered to take her on her initial outing, in this case, for spring gobblers.

"Jim asked me how I would like to go see the sunrise the next morning, hear birds start singing to greet the day, observe flowers in bloom, and maybe even hear a turkey gobble," Sherry recalls. "What's not to like about a morning like that, especially being able to spend it with your husband? I was immediately hooked on hunting."

Similar pleasurable opportunities exist in the fall when deer season comes in, as the leaves are changing, the autumn mornings are refreshingly cool, and migratory songbirds are arriving and leaving.

"I don't know any true outdoorsman who hunts just for the kill," says Sherry. "The experience of being out in nature and getting healthy exercise are other major reasons that both men and women give as answers to why they enjoy hunting."

Crumley says new hunters need mentors, and she suggests that they join organizations such as the NWTF and the Quality Deer Management Association (QDMA) and become involved with local chapters or branches. Lindsay Thomas, director of communications for QDMA, agrees.

"One of the things we strive to do is help our members become students of deer, wildlife, and the habitats they live in," says Thomas. "Members also learn the latest scientific knowledge about how and where deer live and how to hunt and manage them."

In all sincerity, no organization has taught me more about deer hunting and how to manage my land and the game and non-game animals that live there than the QDMA. I am truly grateful for the knowledge that has been imparted to me. Novice hunters, and for that matter, veterans as well, can all benefit from joining a local QDMA branch.

"Our local branch members can be true mentors to new hunters," continues Lindsay. "Branch members can show them where to go hunt, what the local seasons and game laws are, how to field dress and butcher a deer, and how to go about asking landowners for hunting permission, among other things. Novices can build friendships by joining a local branch and really speed up their learning curve on how to be a sportsman and conservationist."

For more information see www.qdma.com. Many states have their own statewide organizations. In my home state, the Virginia Deer Hunters Association is a tremendous resource for new hunters and also a voice for deer enthusiasts. For more information see www.virginiadeerhunters.org.

Most deer hunters begin hunting with a gun, typically a rifle such as a .270 or 30.06. States typically have modern firearms seasons during the rut, which is the period when bucks and does are breeding. Later after these novice hunters have experienced success, they may want to participate in primitive weapon seasons when muzzleloaders or bows (compounds, crossbows, recurves, and longbows) are the designated choices with which deer can be taken.

No matter what season is open, newcomers and veteran hunters should spend a great deal of time sighting in and practicing with their weapon. I hunt with a rifle, muzzleloader, crossbow, and compound, and spend July and August sighting them in.

Since most folks will begin to hunt with a rifle, here's how to sight one in. The same tips would also apply to sighting in a muzzleloader. Also, please wear hearing protection while practicing with a rifle, shotgun, or muzzleloader. I also wear hearing protection while hunting with any kind of gun.

At the store where you purchase the gun, ask someone there to boresight it for you. A boresight device will make sure that when you fire the gun for the first time, the bullet will at least hit the paper target.

Second, go with a mentor to a shooting range or a rural area with a safe backdrop. Place a target 100 yards away from a shooting station, that is, a place where you can rest a gun on pads to make sure that no wobble exists when you fire. Now fire three times, aiming for the bull's-eye. The shots that are fired are called a group.

Third, chances are that your initial group will either be high or low and/or right or left of the bull's-eye. Rifle and muzzleloader scopes have on their tops an elevation adjustment dial (up and down) and on their sides a windage one (left to right.) At 100 yards for both, the Minute of Angle (MOA) will be four clicks per inch. That means, for example, that if your group was three inches low at 100 yards, you would move the elevation dial 12 clicks up.

Next, after you have made the proper adjustments and let the barrel cool a few minutes, which will increase accuracy, shoot another three-shot group until you and your mentor are both satisfied with the results.

Keep in mind that the shot you will be looking for is a deer that is standing still and broadside from you, ideally feeding and at ease. You should aim at an area one-third to one-half up from and behind the back of the front leg shoulder. This is the heart and lung area, often called the boiler room, and it is a fairly large kill zone.

Regardless of what the season is, Sherry urges that hunters, both new and veteran, put into practice the safety rules they learned in classes or from mentors.

"The number one consideration is to always treat a gun as if it were loaded," she says. "Also, identify your target, don't just think that the movement you saw might be a deer. Make sure that a safe backdrop exists behind your target as a bullet can travel a long way. Read your game laws before going afield, so you will know whether bucks or does or other antlerless deer (does and doe and buck fawns are all considered antlerless) are legal on that day, or whether all are legal."

Finding a place to hunt is another aspect that a mentor from organizations such as the QDMA and NWTF can help with. Statistically, says Sherry, not having a place to hunt is the major reason some hunters give up the pastime; again sporting organizations can help newcomers find places to go afield. Generally, people you work with, know socially, or congregate with in places of worship or in clubs are all potential sources that can help novices find access to private land. Federal and state public land, such as national forest and state lands, respectively, are also possible destinations.

Clothing is another consideration. You will need to purchase camouflaged pants, shirt, and jacket made of some sort of non-cotton compound such as polyester. On one of my first hunting trips, I went afield wearing cotton pants and a light jacket. Rain began, the temperature plummeted and before I sulked back down the mountain I had climbed, I was in the early stages of hypothermia. Cotton absorbs moisture, which is a very bad trait for hunting clothing, especially during the general firearms seasons which typically are slated when the temperatures are cooler and precipitation is common.

Under your outer garments, wear several layers of polypropylene or wool underwear. The precise number of layers is determined by how cold the day is. Additional layers of underwear can be kept in a day pack, as can such gear items as a skinning knife, deer drag, flashlights, snacks, water, and hunting licenses. Lastly, you'll need a hat and a blaze orange vest for safety.

My favorite method of deer hunting is stand hunting, which involves sitting for hours in one spot. The two best locales for stand hunting are places where deer come to eat (such as groves where oaks are shedding their acorns) or funnels (places that pinch deer movement so that they must move through certain places to go somewhere to feed or bed down).

Some people who give up on hunting find stand hunting boring—I disagree. I relish listening to and identifying songbirds, mammals, and other creatures, as well as noting what species of trees and shrubs are nearby. While on stand, I also enjoy thinking about how to be a more effective teacher, making plans to do activities with Elaine, and mentally writing stories. While all this is going on in my mind, a deer will often suddenly appear.

This chapter is but a rudimentary introduction to deer hunting. Entire books have been written, for example, on how to kill big Northern bucks during the rut. The more you learn about deer hunting the more you will want to know, and the woods and wildlife will give up their secrets to you slowly but surely.

Before you will cook your venison, of course, you will have to field dress a deer. Field dressing (which means removing the internal organs) takes about five minutes. Here are the basic steps. For dressing all game, it's best to use plastic gloves.

Roll the deer on its back with the rump at your feet. It helps to have the head slightly uphill and the body downhill. I like to place my spread knees on the spread hind legs of the deer to help anchor it. To begin the process, I prefer a 191 Buck Zipper, which features a 4⅛-inch drop point, wide gutting/skinning blade. This is ideal for making the shallow cuts needed so that you don't penetrate internal organs. My friend Paul Hinlicky, who along with his wife Ellen operates St. Gall Farm where they sell honey and meat from grass-fed animals, recommends the following procedure.

Lift up the loose belly skin and make an incision at the bottom of the deer. If it's male, remove the penis and testicles by grabbing and lifting them from the bottom. Then sever from the carcass and discard.

Then insert the zipper edge of the knife and slowly pull it from the pelvic area all the way along the center line of the carcass up to the neck. Be sure to cut shallowly, keeping the blade above the stomach and intestines. Paul likes to skin the stomach side deer of the deer at this point.

Insert the straight edge of the knife under the breastbone, and, keeping it flat against the rib cage, cut tight toward the back to both ends. This severs the diaphragm (the thin internal membrane that divides the stomach from the heart and lungs). Again, be careful not to cut into internal organs, especially the stomach and intestines.

At this point with your left hand, lift up the stomach and intestines and with your right hand, put the knife inside the cavity up the backbone as far as you can reach. Pulling with the left hand and cutting with the right, separate the ligaments holding the stomach and the intestines to the cavity. As you do this a few inches at a time, the stomach and intestines will begin to fall away from the cavity. As you reach the pelvic area, separate the bladder by cutting the "piping" that goes to the penis. Be careful not to spill the bladder.

Next, reach into the upper chest cavity, grab the heart/lung area with your left hand and with knife in your right hand, sever the connecting tissue and extract these organs. Flip the deer over and let its blood drain.

Collect the organ meat that you want to save such as the heart, liver, tongue, and kidneys. Paul saves the lungs, boils them, and feeds them to his chickens. When Paul brings the carcass home, he uses a hacksaw to split the pelvic shield over the urinary tract and extracts what remains of the intestinal tissue, being careful not to spill feces on the meat. He cuts the esophagus from the neck and flushes the interior of the carcass with water until all blood and debris, such as leaves or dirt, are removed.

Paul prefers to butcher all his deer, while Elaine and I butcher several of ours annually, taking the rest to a professional butcher.

2. Venison Recipes

We feel that venison is the healthiest red meat. For example, *organic* is a much used word today, but deer hunters are the original organic food eaters as this animal is cage-free, chemical-free, and a true natural food. Venison is extremely good for your health as it is a superb source of protein, low in fat (especially saturated fat), and a fine source of iron, Vitamin B12, riboflavin, niacin, and Vitamin B6.

Sweet Venison Stew

What puts the "sweet" in Sweet Venison Stew is the generous helping of sweet potatoes. We think you'll find that deer burger has never had a better significant other.

Ingredients

1	pound ground venison
2–3	raw sweet potatoes
1	medium onion
1	28-oz. can diced tomatoes
6	medium carrots
1–2	cups grated cabbage
½	cup chopped celery
3	cups vegetable broth (if possible use organic, and use it full strength)
1	bay leaf
½	tsp thyme
¼	tsp basil
1	garlic clove
	Salt and pepper to taste
2	Tbsp Dulse flakes, optional (this seaweed adds the boost of vitamins B6, B12, iron and folate. It can be found in many health food stores).

Directions

Mince the garlic, allowing it to sit 5–10 minutes before use. Chop the onion. Brown the venison, onion, and garlic in a stock pot. Peel the potatoes and dice them into 1-inch chunks.

To the venison, mix/add the sweet potatoes, carrots, cabbage, chopped celery, canned tomatoes, and vegetable broth. Bring to a boil in a stove pot and add salt and pepper as desired. Reduce heat and simmer for at least one hour.

Sweet Venison Stew goes well with a tossed salad and cornbread.

Enjoy!

Mediterranean Venison

This recipe was suggested by Tonya Triplett, sales manager for the Abingdon (Virginia) Convention and Visitors Bureau. We borrowed part of her recipe, added ingredients of our own, experimented some more, and finally devised the following recipe. A key is high quality olive oil; the Abingdon Olive Oil Company, which we visited during our sojourn, offered the best olive oil we have ever used. And as always, we relish cooking on our 10-inch cast iron skillet. We use Camp Chef cast iron pots and skillets, but many other quality manufacturers are available, including Le Creuset, Calphalon, Lodge, Tramontina, and MACA

Ingredients

2	lbs venison steak
3	Tbsp gourmet olive oil — (we prefer Milanese Gremolata, a fused olive oil)
1–2	Tbsp balsamic vinegar — (we chose Pomegranate Balsamic Vinegar, a dark, sweet variety)
2	garlic cloves, minced
2	cups broth — (we prefer organic chicken broth)

Directions

Cover the steak with the Milanese Gremolata Olive Oil, Pomegranate Balsamic Vinegar, and garlic. Allow to marinate for at least 4 hours, and perhaps as long as 12.

Add more Milanese Gremolata Olive Oil to cover the bottom of a cast iron skillet. Heat the oil over medium and brown the steak lightly on both sides.

Cover the browned steak with broth. Bring to a boil, then reduce heat to low and cover with a lid. Cook over low approximately 4 hours. Tonya Triplett suggests drizzling with olive oil (she prefers Wild Mushroom and Sage) half way through the cooking. Add more broth as necessary. If desired, add mushrooms and mild onions an hour before cooking concludes.

Serve with such favorite Mediterranean vegetables as asparagus, red onions, mushrooms, tomatoes, and either zucchini or squash.

Enjoy!

"Butternutty" Venison Pot Roast

Pot roast is a traditional Southern meal with beef as the main ingredient, usually accompanied by the standard potatoes and onions. But if you want to move beyond standard to scrumptious, substitute venison for beef, add butternut squash as a major player, and cook everything in a cast iron pot.

For this dish, we prefer a 10" cast iron pot, partially for its reputation, durability, and ease of use, but also for the fact that we can cook an entire meal in it, gaining the tenderness and flavor that cast iron cooking adds. The key, of course, is the slow cooking process that enhances the flavor of the venison roast.

Prepare a 2-lb venison roast by removing as much silver skin and fat as possible.

Place the roast in a self-sealing bag and marinade for 12–24 hours in the following mixture.

Ingredients

3	Tbsp red wine vinegar
2	Tbsp lemon juice
1–2	tsp Worcestershire sauce
2	Tbsp olive oil
5	crushed garlic cloves
½	tsp ground cinnamon
5	whole cloves
½	tsp salt
¼	tsp ground pepper

Directions

About 3 hours before cooking, remove the meat from the marinade and allow it to drain.

In a cast iron pot, heat 2 Tbsp canola oil on medium. Brown the meat on all sides in the oil.

On top of the browned meat, place ½ of a medium sliced onion and 2 celery stalks cut into 3-inch pieces. Pour 2 cups of broth over the meat and vegetables — we use organic vegetable broth, but beef broth, chicken stock, or game stock would all work well. Reduce the heat and simmer, covered, for 2 hours.

Prepare a butternut squash by peeling, removing the seeds (a grapefruit spoon is helpful for this part) and cutting the squash into 1-inch chunks. Add these chunks to the venison dish after it has cooked for two hours. Replace the lid and cook for another hour, or until the squash is tender.

Enjoy!

Venison Sloppy Joes

Ingredients

1	lb ground venison burger
2	Tbsp olive oil
½	green pepper, chopped (Some folks prefer red pepper for extra "punch," but Bruce is allergic to red peppers, thus we opt for the green version.)
½	red onion, chopped
2	cloves garlic, minced
1	stalk celery, chopped
1	15-oz. can tomato sauce (We use a pint jar of home-canned tomato sauce, made from garden tomatoes.)
2	Tbsp brown sugar
2	tsp apple cider vinegar
1	Tbsp Worcestershire sauce
1–2	Tbsp yellow mustard
	Salt and pepper to taste (We prefer sea salt and ground black pepper for extra flavor.)

Directions

Heat a cast iron skillet on medium. Pour in the olive oil. Add the ground venison and let it start to brown.

As the venison browns, add the green pepper, onion, celery, and garlic. Let it cook until tender and until the meat is fully browned.

Add the tomato sauce, brown sugar, vinegar, Worcestershire sauce, and mustard. Stir well and allow mixture to cook 20–30 minutes to thicken. You may have to lower the heat to allow it to simmer without scorching. Add salt and pepper as desired.

Serve on whole wheat buns. Makes 5–6 sandwiches.

Enjoy!

Venison sloppy joes may be a little messy to eat,
but after one bite you won't care.

Venison Guláš (Goulash)

Friend Paul Hinlicky is of Slovakian heritage. His wife Ellen shared this recipe (and its history) with us. In that part of the world, the *jelen* is a common Slovak deer that's hunted for food and is typically the main part of this recipe.

"Central Europeans love stews, bits of meat cooked slowly in liquid, as a way to tenderize their sometimes tough and stringy meat," says Ellen. "A typical lunchtime meal in Slovakia, Hungary, or the Czech Republic is chicken soup with noodles (lunch always begins with soup); then a plate of meat stew with potatoes, rice, or dumplings; and dessert. This is a brilliant way to make a little bit of food go as far as possible, and strengthens a hungry laborer for the long afternoon, especially when a six-o'clock breakfast consists of a salami sandwich and a bottle of beer."

Ellen says that she and Paul first enjoyed this goulash (or guláš as it's known in Slovak) many years ago in the Western Slovak town of Nitra.

"I remember this goulash especially for its complex blend of both sweet and hot paprika," she says. "Ideally, a stew of this type is cooked in a heavy cast-iron pot over an open fire; the flavor is incomparably better for being exposed to a live fire and smoke, but an excellent version can also be cooked in a heavy kettle on a modern stove."

Ellen adds that Slovaks often prepare goulash in their cottages in the mountains. The goulash recipe also works equally well outdoors with a Dutch oven and indoors with a cast iron pot.

Ingredients

10	ounces venison, steaks, roasts, or neck meat, trimmed of all fat and sinew and cut into 1-inch cubes
1	large onion, peeled and diced
1	tsp salt, ¼ tsp black pepper, 2 tsp sweet paprika and ¼ tsp hot paprika, mixed together well in a small bowl
4	cups boiling water
2	Tbsp tomato paste
2	slices black bread, crusts removed and cut into small squares

Directions

Soften the onion in cooking oil, but don't let it brown. Add the meat cubes, the salt-seasoning mix, and toss together. Immediately pour in three cups of boiling water. Heat slowly, till barely simmering; cook, covered, over low heat for an hour. Then add the remaining cup of water and the black bread squares, which lend flavor and thickening to the sauce. Cook till the meat is tender, one half to one hour more.

Barbecued Venison

We also received this suggestion from Ellen Hinlicky. Ellen wrote that a friend, while she and Paul were living in New York State, often served this entrée to great acclaim. A cast iron pot is ideal for cooking this dish.

Ingredients

3	lbs boneless venison, cubed
	Flour, salt, pepper
3	onions, sliced

Directions

Dredge the venison in seasoned flour, and place in a cast iron pot or other heavy roasting pan such as a Dutch oven that has been lightly coated with oil (no browning of the meat is necessary). Cover the meat cubes with the sliced onion and add salt and pepper. Then add a sauce mixed from the following.

¾	cup ketchup
2	Tbsp vinegar
2	Tbsp soy sauce
2	Tbsp Worcestershire sauce
2	Tbsp prepared mustard (we added the mustard, feeling that it counterbalances the overall sweetness of the sauce, plus we like the additional flavor that the mustard brings)
½	cup brown sugar
¾	cup warm water

Bake, covered, for three hours at 250°F. Serve on hot rice or noodles. Ellen prefers this dish with rice and so do we. Also, readers may enjoy venison barbecue on whole wheat or other buns.

Enjoy!

Company's Coming Venison Burgers

We obtained a combination burner grill and stove as the perfect device for power outages, camping, and deer camps. We've had our daughter Sarah, her husband David, and son Sam over for a cookout, and found the grill was also ideal for cooking venison burgers and marinated squash and pepper slices.

When we began thinking about Company's Coming Venison Burgers, the biggest hurdle was how to keep them tasting moist. For health reasons, we choose not to add fat to our venison as it is being ground, and since the meat is already lean, sometimes dryness can occur. We think we have found a solution and are pleased with the result. Hope you will be, too.

Ingredients

3	lb ground venison
½	cup bread crumbs
2	beaten eggs
½	cup diced onion
1	minced garlic clove
1–2	Tbsp Worcestershire sauce
	Salt and pepper to taste

Directions

Combine the ingredients in a bowl and mix thoroughly with your hands. Form into patties.

About ½ hour before grilling, caramelize onions for a burger topper. Heat 2 Tbsp olive oil in a skillet. Slice one large sweet onion and add to the skillet, cooking on low to allow the onions to sweat and begin to caramelize. After about 15 minutes, add 4–5 sliced mushrooms to the onions and continue cooking for another 15 minutes or so.

When the onions and mushrooms seem tender, grill the burger patties to their desired doneness. Top with sharp cheddar cheese slices and the mushroom/onion mixture.

A good side dish is grilled yellow squash and red bell pepper. Slice the vegetables into a bowl and toss with bottled Italian dressing. Grill until tender.

Enjoy!

No Power-No Problem-Venison with Cabbage

Every winter, we lose electric power for various lengths of time at our home. One June, high winds knocked us off the grid for 48 hours, and of course, like many folks, we are always looking for ways to cook and serve meals while camping.

A possible solution for all these sans electricity times is a combination burner grill and stove designed for outdoor use and fired by small propane tanks.

For us, the goal is to be able to cook a one-pot meal on our grill/stove combo that will use basic pantry ingredients and items most likely on hand during a power outage, and to create a meal that would not require a long cooking time. Additionally the meal will provide a good balance of food groups without the necessity of multiple dishes, a consideration when without power, or in the field. Our choice is an easy version of stuffed cabbage with venison, and without the labor of the "stuffed" method.

Ingredients

1	Tbsp canola oil
1	lb ground venison
1	medium onion, chopped
3	cloves minced garlic
1	32 oz. jar spaghetti sauce
3	Tbsp fresh parsley, chopped
1	tsp dried oregano
1	tsp sugar
½	tsp salt
¼	tsp pepper
½	head shredded cabbage, or a 10-oz bag of shredded cabbage ready for coleslaw

Heat the oil in a 10-inch cast iron pot. Add the venison and cook 5 to 6 minutes, until no longer pink. Add the chopped onions and cook 4 to 5 minutes until tender. Add garlic and cook a minute longer. Add spaghetti sauce and seasonings. Simmer 5 minutes, then add shredded cabbage. Cook covered, until cabbage is tender, about 8 to 10 minutes. Serves 6. Use the grill to toast bread slices or to cook slices of yellow squash tossed in olive oil and minced garlic.

Enjoy!

Pan Seared Venison Tenderloin

This entrée is easy and quick to prepare, but several things are key.

- Properly tenderize venison tenderloin, done by either yourself or your butcher.
- Allow plenty of time for the meat to marinade and use quality rub.
- Quality cast iron cookery.
- Don't overcook.

If you do these things, Pan Seared Venison Tenderloin is the ideal "fancy meal" for treasured friends. We suggest serving with stir fried summer squash and onions, hot homemade biscuits, and perhaps a wild fruit pie.

Ingredients

1–2	lb venison tenderloin
4	Tbsp olive oil per lb
2	Tbsp white vinegar per lb
1	package marinade seasoning of your choice—we prefer Soy Ginger. Also this dish works equally well using Garlic Pepper Rub.

Directions

Slice the tenderloin into portions ½–¾ inches thick and 2 inches long. Tenderize the tenderloin with a meat mallet or other tenderizing tool.

Combine 2 Tbsp marinade mix, 4 Tbsp olive oil, and 2 Tbsp white vinegar for each pound of meat. Stir until well mixed. (Or use Garlic Pepper Rub in place of the marinade mix, still using the oil and vinegar.)

Place the meat in a zip-lock bag and cover with the marinade.

Allow to sit in the refrigerator for several hours, or even better, overnight.

Heat a skillet over medium heat. Add 1 Tbsp olive oil. When heated, place the slices of tenderloin in the skillet so that they are not touching one another, and brown slightly on one side—2 to 3 minutes. Turn and briefly cook on the other side, 1 to 2 minutes. Watch carefully or the tenderloin will overcook.

Baked Venison Burgers

Ingredients

1	lb of venison burger
1	egg
2	tsp yellow mustard
1	Tbsp marinade seasoning
¼	tsp Garlic Pepper Rub seasonings
2	slices whole wheat bread turned into crumbs

Directions

Marinade the venison overnight in the seasonings.

Mix 1-pound burger with egg, yellow mustard, and whole wheat bread crumbs.

Form into patties and place into aluminum pan.

Bake 20–25 minutes at 400°F. The burgers will be done when their internal temperature reaches 160°F.

Notes

The egg and bread crumbs help hold the patties together and also help keep them moist.

We prefer to lightly sprinkle the Garlic Pepper Rub on the meat so as not to overpower the venison flavor.

A minute or so before we remove the patties from the oven, we place strips of sharp cheddar cheese on the patties.

Fix-Ahead Venison Cube Steak

This is a good recipe when you don't have time to be in the kitchen just before a meal, or when it is too hot to cook. A slow cooker makes preparation easy.

Ingredients

2	lbs cubed venison steak
1	medium sweet onion, cut into chunks
3	carrots, sliced in 1-inch pieces

⅔	cup catsup
⅔	cup water
½	cup brown sugar
2	tsp yellow mustard
1	envelope dry onion soup mix

Place the venison steaks in the bottom of the slow cooker. Cover with the onion chunks. Combine the remaining ingredients in a bowl and pour over the venison and onions.

Cover and cook on low for 5–6 hours. This dish has a stew-like consistency that would go well on top of rice or pasta. You could add other items in as well, such as potatoes, mushrooms, or peas.

Italian Style Venison Meatloaf

The first time Elaine told me she was going to prepare venison meatloaf, I was not happy. As a boy, I recall meatloaf as being a dish that was one of my least favorite meals and that had to be smothered in ketchup to be made tolerable. After a brief protest by yours truly, Elaine convinced me that Italian Style Venison Meatloaf would cook up great in a loaf pan. And she was right.

Ingredients

1½	cups whole wheat bread cubes
1	cup milk
1½	lbs ground venison
1	medium carrot
2–3	garlic cloves
1	medium onion
1	cup frozen spinach, thawed
1	cup grated Parmesan/Romano blend grated cheese
⅓	cup marinara sauce
2	tsp dried parsley or ¼ cup chopped fresh parsley
2	tsp dried oregano
1½	tsp kosher salt
3	eggs

Directions

Place the bread cubes in a small bowl and cover with the milk. Soak for 30 minutes.

While the bread soaks, combine the carrot, garlic, onion, spinach, and marinara sauce in a food processor and process until all large pieces are fine and all is well blended.

In a large bowl combine the venison, cheese, parsley, oregano, salt, eggs, mixture from the food processor, and softened bread cubes which have been well-drained. Mix all ingredients thoroughly with your hands.

Shape the mixture into a ring on a baking sheet. Place, uncovered, in a 375 degree oven and bake for approximately 45 minutes. Then cover the top thoroughly with 1–1½ cups more marinara sauce, even putting some in the center of the ring. Return to the oven, uncovered, and bake a further 45 minutes.

Let stand 5 minutes or so before serving. This goes well over brown rice.

Venison Pastitsio

Ingredients

	Tomato-Meat Sauce
3	Tbsp olive oil
1	large yellow onion, chopped
2	lb ground venison
3	cloves garlic, minced
2	tsp cinnamon
1	tsp dried oregano
1	tsp fresh thyme leaves
1	15-oz. can diced tomatoes
1	15-oz. can tomato sauce
2	tsp salt and 1 tsp pepper
	Bechamel sauce
1½	cups of 2 % milk
1	cup half and half
4	Tbsp butter
¼	cup flour
¼	tsp grated nutmeg
1½	cups grated Parmesan cheese

2	eggs, beaten
⅔	cup plain Greek yogurt
¾	lb pasta shells
1	tsp salt and 1 tsp pepper

Directions

Heat the olive oil in a large pot.

Sauté the onions 5 minutes, then add ground venison and brown it until no longer pink, about 10 minutes.

Add the garlic, cinnamon, oregano, and thyme. Cook over medium heat 5 minutes.

Add the tomatoes, tomato sauce, salt and pepper. Simmer for 40–45 minutes.

Preheat the oven to 350°F. While the oven is preheating, prepare the Bechamel sauce as follows.

Heat the milk and cream together in a saucepan until simmering.

In a separate medium saucepan, melt the butter.

Add the flour and cook over medium until the flour turns tan, meanwhile whisking constantly for 3–4 minutes.

Pour the warm milk-cream mixture into the butter, whisking constantly. Cook over medium for 5 to 7 minutes, stirring frequently, until thick and smooth.

Add nutmeg, salt, and pepper.

Stir in ¾ cup of Parmesan cheese, and ½ cup of the tomato-meat sauce. Let this mixture cool for 10 minutes, then stir in the eggs and yogurt and set aside.

Meanwhile, cook the pasta in a large pot until tender but not overcooked because the pasta will continue to cook as it bakes. Drain and set aside.

Add the pasta to the remaining meat sauce and pour into a 9- by 13-inch baking dish. Spread the Bechamel sauce over the meat and pasta, covering evenly. Sprinkle with the remaining ¾ cup Parmesan cheese.

Bake for 1 hour until golden brown. Cool for 10 minutes before serving.

Note: Serves 8

Enjoy!

Venison Chicken Brunswick Stew

Traditionally, cooks have paired venison with a number of other meats, but especially with chicken. And traditionally, hunters have regarded Brunswick stew, often simmered for hours in a Dutch oven or cast iron pot while the hunters were afield, as a scrumptious fortifier after a long day.

Note: we found 10-inch cast iron pot ideal for cooking the amounts listed for the below recipe. If you have a large group to prepare for, double the ingredients and try a 21 quart canning pot (or equivalent).

Ingredients

1	2–3 lb chicken
1	lb ground venison
1	15-oz. can baby lima beans, undrained
1	28-oz. can diced tomatoes
1	10-oz. bag frozen baby lima beans
2	medium potatoes, peeled and diced
1	medium yellow onion, diced
½	cup catsup
1	15-oz. can cream style corn
2	Tbsp sugar
2	Tbsp butter
1½	tsp salt
½	tsp pepper
1	tsp hot sauce, optional

Directions

Cover the chicken with water and cook with lid on pot for 1 hour, until meat falls from the bone. Remove the chicken and carcass and set aside. Reserve 2 cups of broth for the stew and return it to the pot.

Pour the canned lima beans through a strainer and reserve the beans, adding the liquid to the broth in the pot. Add the tomatoes to the broth. Bring these ingredients to a boil over medium heat and cook, stirring often, until liquid is reduced by about one-third. While this is reducing, remove the chicken meat from the bones and shred for later use.

Puree the reserved beans and add them to the reduced broth, along with two cups of the shredded chicken, the ground venison (crumbled but still raw), catsup, frozen lima beans, diced potatoes, and diced onion. Cover and cook over low heat about 3 ½ hours, stirring often.

Add the canned corn, sugar, butter, salt, and pepper and cook over low heat for one more hour. Adding hot sauce at this time is optional, depending on how much kick you like.

Good with biscuits or cornbread.

Enjoy!

Venison Stroganoff

This recipe comes courtesy of Maryanne and Lee Walker of Glen Allen, Virginia. Maryanne hails from Switzerland and this entrée reflects her heritage, whereas Lee, who is the Virginia Game Department's Outreach Director, is an avid deer hunter.

"Just about any stroganoff recipe can be adapted to using venison," says Maryanne. "I also prefer to use German-style Spätzle noodles."

We made a few adjustments to the Walker's recipe to reflect our tastes. Maryanne's noodles tasted great, but "regular" noodles or even brown rice performs well, too.

Ingredients

1	lb venison steak cut into strips
4	Tbsp olive oil
4	Tbsp butter
⅓	cup Vidalia onion, sliced
8	oz. Portabella mushrooms, sliced
½	tsp Worcestershire sauce
1	cup buttermilk
2	cups flour
¼	tsp garlic powder
½	tsp sea salt
¼	tsp ground pepper
½	cup sour cream
1 to 1½	cups chicken broth
	Bag of noodles or four servings of brown rice

Directions

In a small bowl combine the flour, garlic powder, salt, and pepper. In another bowl place the buttermilk.

Dredge the venison strips in the flour mixture, then in the buttermilk. Return them to the flour mixture a second time.

Heat the oil in a pot and brown over medium heat. Add the broth and Worcestershire sauce, cover, and simmer for an hour or so.

In a separate skillet cook the onions and mushrooms until tender. Add the onions and mushrooms to the simmering venison at the end of the hour. Add salt and pepper to taste. Remove from heat and stir in the sour cream, not allowing the mixture to heat as high as when simmering or the sour cream will curdle.

Serve over noodles, the traditional choice, or our pick of brown rice.

Venison Roast Sandwiches

When on a fishing or hunting trip or for school lunches, I really like roast venison sandwiches. They are very filling, plus low in calories and high in protein. I pack two in a small cooler with an ice block and am good to go. Here is Elaine's recipe.

Directions

1	Venison Roast
1	can cream of mushroom soup
	Assorted vegetables for flavor, especially onions, carrots, and potatoes. These vegetables can be placed in a separate container for the trip or eaten later at home.

Place venison roast in slow cooker
Add 1 can of soup and 1 can of water to cover meat
Add vegetables
Cover, cook for 6 to 8 hours or until meat is tender.
Enjoy!

Sarah's Venison Sausage Chili with Sweet Potatoes

When our daughter Sarah invited us over for a venison Sunday dinner with her husband David Reynolds and their two sons Sam and Eli, she only requested that we bring one item: our cast iron pot. That was enough to lure us, along with the promise of homemade strawberry pie for dessert.

What Sarah whipped up was a chili entrée mild enough to suit the tastes of our three-year-old and 11-month-old grandsons, yet zesty enough to rate huzzahs from the adults in the room. And the strawberry pie proved to be a perfect complement.

Elaine preparing venison chili in a slow cooker.

Venison Sausage Chili with Sweet Potatoes

Ingredients

2–3	sweet potatoes
	Olive oil
1	lb mild venison sausage
1	small onion, chopped
1	15-oz. can black beans, drained and rinsed
1	15-oz. can peeled, crushed tomatoes
2–3	cups beef broth
1	tsp cumin
⅛	tsp chili powder
1½–2	tsp Jamaican jerk seasoning
	Sea salt
	Ground pepper

Directions

At least 1 ½ hours before cooking the chili, peel the sweet potatoes and cut into cubes. Toss them gently with a drizzle of olive oil, and season to taste with sea salt and ground pepper. Spread the cubes on a baking sheet and roast in the oven at 425°F for about 1 to 1¼ hours, until they are soft. You may do the roasting earlier in the day if you choose.

Into the cast iron pot, pour about 1 Tbsp olive oil and heat over medium. Add the chopped onions and cook 5–6 minutes, until tender.

Next add the mild venison sausage and cook until browned. Pour in the bean, tomatoes, roasted sweet potatoes, beef broth, cumin, chili powder, and Jamaican jerk seasoning. Cook over medium heat for about 20 minutes, until the flavors have time to marry.

Deer Heart: A Delicacy for Sure

As someone who depends on venison for almost all the red meat Elaine and I need, and who tries to kill ten whitetails annually to fulfill those needs, I regard the consumption of venison as part of a healthy, active lifestyle. I would even speculate that we probably dine on a venison dish of some kind well over 300 days a year. So it might surprise some venison aficionados that one of our favorite parts of a deer is an organ that most people throw away—the heart, which Elaine and I regard as a delicacy.

Many years ago, I began to feel guilty about all the organs abandoned in the woods after the field dressing had been completed. Elaine and I talked to other hunters, conducted some research on the Internet, and decided that the heart would be our first culinary project from among the various organs.

From our inquiries, Elaine and I found that deer hearts are most often fried with onions. For health reasons, we generally avoid frying any food, but in this case, we found fried deer heart a little too tough for our taste and also that the onions and other ingredients obscured the flavor of the organ.

Elaine then decided to put the heart in a slow cooker with a can of Cream of Mushroom soup. The result was incredibly scrumptious and is generally the manner which we have dined on this organ ever since. Specifically, Elaine prefers the soup. While I do enjoy heart cooked in soup, I most often just cover the organ with water.

All we do to cook the heart is simmer it in a slow cooker for five or so hours. After cooking and then chilling the organ overnight, we slice it thin, slather mustard on whole wheat bread, and add some sharp cheddar cheese. An average size heart can produce enough meat for four or five lunches.

Cooked in this manner, the heart boasts a delicate—dare I say slightly sweet—flavor that is nutritious as well as tasty. The mustard and sharp cheddar enhance the flavor instead of overwhelming it.

After the scrumptious success of this recipe, we next turned to cooking the liver, albeit with extremely disappointing results. We first tried the classic liver and onions repast. The entrée smelled enticing on the stovetop, the first bite tasted fine, the second not so much, and by the third we decided we could not finish our meal. The overpowering flavor of a deer's liver was just too much for us.

We then tried baking a liver loaf in the oven and disliked that dish even more than the previous one. After just one bite, we were finished eating. We gave the rest of the loaf to a friend who after trying the dish told us that he likewise was only able to swallow (barely) one bite.

Give deer heart a try, you won't regret it. Here's another heart recipe of Elaine's.

Venison Heart Stew

Ingredients

1	venison heart, cleaned and cut into cubes
½	small can of diced tomatoes
2	small potatoes, peeled and cubed
2	carrots, sliced
½	small onion cut into chunks
1	minced garlic clove
1	cup fresh or frozen lima beans
⅓	cup peeled and diced turnip
½	cup diced mushrooms
1	cup broth (try using broth from deer bone marrow)
¼–½	tsp dried basil
3	juniper berries
	Salt and pepper to taste

Directions

Combine all ingredients in a cast iron Dutch oven. Cover and simmer over low heat for 3 to 4 hours.

Any other vegetables can be added as desired.

Deer Tongue Salad

Our next item to experiment with was the tongue—rather I should say I began to try it out, as Elaine just couldn't bring herself to taste this organ. My reasoning was that in the 1800s, Americans regarded buffalo tongue as a delicacy and it became a high dollar entrée in the country's best restaurants. So why wouldn't a deer's prove to be equally scrumptious?

I slow-cooked my first deer tongue and found it to be tough and unappetizing—thus ending the research on that potential menu item. But after reflection and while reading about cooking animal organs, I discovered that mammal tongues have a sheath around them that must be peeled, which I had not done on my initial kitchen test.

Deer Tongue salad is a great choice for a workaday
lunch — and a sure conversation starter.

Intrigued about trying tongue again, I again slow-cooked this organ and sliced it into small pieces, consuming it on brown bread with sharp cheddar cheese and mustard — the same way I prefer heart. And the tongue was quite tasty, possessing a milder flavor than heart but nevertheless very appealing and featuring a somewhat "light, delicate" taste.

Experimenting again, I found that deer tongue, as the prime player, makes an excellent salad.

In a slow cooker, cook the tongue on high for three hours. I've removed the sheath immediately after cooking and after refrigeration... the latter approach works better.

On top of a bed of spinach, thinly slice the chilled tongue and add sharp cheddar cheese, black walnuts, cranberries, and avocado bits — my favorite add-ons. Feel free to experiment with your favorite vegetables and cheeses.

Unusual Venison Dishes

People often are fascinated by almost anything having to do with deer, and for some—perhaps many—of us that enthrallment extends to the eating of various parts of this mammal.

Perhaps the most unusual recipe we have encountered comes courtesy of James Hancock, a professional wildlife habitat manager who operates Virginia Wildlife and Land Management and is vice president of the Roanoke, Virginia branch of the Quality Deer Management Association.

"Years ago, my girlfriend at the time, Jessica Kane, was of Scottish descent," recalls James. "We go deer hunting and Jessica kills her first deer. She's very excited and immediately declares that she wants to make venison haggis for the two of us. I didn't object but I admit that I had concerns. I'm just not a huge organ eater, but I did like the idea of using more of the animal."

For those unfamiliar with this traditional Scottish dish, haggis often consists of various organs (think liver, heart, tongue, kidneys, and perhaps even the lungs) boiled and minced, then placed in a large bowl. Then add suet, onions, and oats or oatmeal as well as salt, pepper, and various herbs. This conglomeration is then placed inside the stomach, which is sewed or tied shut. Some chefs boil the stomach, others bake it.

"So we take the deer's stomach, rinse it out, and stuff the diced liver, kidneys, and heart inside, then mix in some oats and sew up the entire stomach like some sort of big cooking bag," continues James.

"When the stomach comes out of the oven, the thing has shrunk and taken on a texture resembling a large loaf of bread. The stomach looks very crispy on the outside, not at all tough, just like a crust of bread."

Nevertheless, James remains skeptical about eating the haggis, but also, he says, concerned about hurting Jessica's feelings and wary too of the "fiery redhead's Scottish temper."

"I decide to eat a few bites, proclaim them delicious, and slip the rest to the dog when Jessica isn't looking," says James. "But to my surprise, the haggis is really quite good. We end up having a great meal and enjoying the leftovers the next day. The oats gave the dish a rich taste and also tamped down the liver flavor. I also can state that I have never eaten anything that I could compare the taste of deer haggis to."

Marrow at Mealtime

James, who was born and raised in Virginia, lived for many years out West as a hunting and fishing guide and has been exposed to many kinds of wild game dishes. He recalls that a good Western friend of his evinced a fondness for any kind of soup that came partially from stock made from the marrow of deer bones. The man merely scraped out the marrow and stored it until ready to make stock. Some folks like to bake and/or boil the bones, then remove the marrow.

Although Americans seem to have little affinity for bone marrow, many cultures, including Native Americans, have long taken advantage of the nutritional benefits. Marrow is high in Vitamin A, omega 3 fatty acids, and contains calcium, iron, phosphorous, and many other nutrients as well. Try experimenting with some bone marrow the next time you kill a whitetail.

Indeed, Paul Hinlicky, of Catawba, Virginia, fondly recalls consuming soup made from deer bone marrow.

"My mom was of Slavic origin, and in Europe it is very common to eat soup made from the marrow of the native deer," he says. "My mom's standard approach was to slice the bone at an angle so that the marrow would leach out into the pot. Mom would also leave meat and gristle, especially if they were tough, on the bone.

"She would simmer all this for hours, periodically skimming anything that came to the surface of the mixture. What would be left was very clear broth, and the tough meat and gristle became very soft. Mom then put noodles and various vegetables and herbs into the broth which became a very tasty soup. And the leftover, now-tender meat could be put into the soup or eaten separately. It was all quite good."

Ribs as a Repast

I try to kill ten deer and four or five turkeys from various states every year, as Elaine and I have made a commitment to eat wild game meat instead of the supermarket version. Because of time constraints, we usually only butcher a few of the whitetails. None of the butchers we have brought deer to over the years would consent to cutting out the ribs for us, saying it was too much work. I asked Paul, who butchers all of the deer he kills annually, if it is difficult to remove the ribs.

"It's a shame that more hunters don't use the rib meat because it is not too hard to remove the ribs," he says. "The ribs attach to the breast bone and spine.

After you quarter a deer and have removed the loins, hams, and shoulder and neck meat, place what is left of the deer on a table. Then take a hack saw and cut the ribs from the breast bone and spine. I find it a little harder to remove the ribs from the breast bone than the spine, but not all that difficult really."

Afterwards, continues Paul, the ribs can be cooked several different ways. The Virginian's favorite way is to slather barbecue sauce on the ribs and slow cook this entrée outdoors and inside a covered grill. After about 45 minutes, begin checking the ribs for tenderness.

"Barbecued deer ribs are mild tasting and quite tender," says Paul.

Deer Lungs Anyone?

I was not able to find anyone who had eaten deer lungs, but Paul Hinlicky does offer a way for folks to use this organ.

"My chickens love deer lungs," he said. "Put the lungs, or any other organ you don't want, into a pot filled half way with water. Boil for 15 to 20 minutes, then grind and freeze the mixture. Every time I want to give a treat to my chickens, I thaw some portion of the mixture and give it to them."

Pet dogs and cats may also find deer lungs palatable.

Deer Heart

I love deer heart (see earlier recipes) and so do other folks. Scot Sutherland, an avid deer hunter from Roanoke, Virginia says that he prefers deer heart for breakfast. Scot browns the heart (sliced and in small chunks) in a skillet with butter, then makes an omelet with four eggs, green peppers, onions, garlic, salt, and pepper. This dish serves two.

Liver Loaf Anyone?

Goodness knows Elaine and I have tried to like/eat/swallow deer liver but, frankly, have failed miserably. We've tried the traditional route of fried liver and onions, and we've attempted to bake this organ (liver loaf anyone?)—all to no avail. I confess that we like the robust smell of liver cooking in the kitchen. And when the dish is done, the first bite is always good, the second one not so much, and the third creates the disagreeable sensation that we have swallowed the proverbial lead pipe. Furthermore, I have shared our liver recipes and entrées with various relatives and friends; the response from the latter has been that if we want to continue to have them as friends — no more liver dishes.

Elaine now refuses to taste or prepare liver, and though I am still game to try another method of cooking (without my spouse's approval or help) my desire to do so is, well, exceptionally weak. I have heard of folks making liver palatable by first soaking it in milk or water with a generous amount of lemon juice; maybe this season, or in a few seasons, I will try one of those approaches.

Scot Sutherland says he grew up eating deer liver, prepared enthusiastically by his father in a frying pan with the requisite onions, salt, and pepper.

"I never liked it, though," says Scott. "The meat had a mushy, granular texture and as I would slide it around on the plate, dad would say 'What's wrong with you, boy.' Today, I put diced deer liver in a skillet, cover it with water, and boil it for about 20 minutes. My dogs love it."

Kidneys

One of my goals is to try deer kidneys. From my research, I've learned that this organ must be soaked in a bowl of water overnight to remove the urine smell and taste. I've read, though I could locate no one who has actually tried deer kidneys, that this organ goes well with scrambled eggs and as part of the traditional British dish: kidney pudding. I have also read that kidneys have an even more powerful flavor than liver, which could give some folks pause to try this organ.

But not me. Perhaps I'll have a future story that will sing the praises of the kidney. And for the truly adventurous folks, there's always deer tripe and chitterlings. For the uninformed, tripe is the stomach and chitterlings are the fried intestines. However, Elaine and I are not quite ready to make a culinary leap of faith in the direction of those two organs.

3. Getting Started on Turkey Hunting

In 1986, Jim Clay, who operates Perfection Turkey Calls, took me on my first turkey hunt. Jim simultaneously called in three jakes (young male turkeys); and in my nervousness, I shot at and missed all three. Although Jim was very kind and encouraging to me after my blunder, I was humiliated and silently vowed to become a competent turkey hunter one day.

Doing so took me years. The same will likely be true for any beginner of any age. For me, turkeys are the most fascinating animal in the woods, possessing superior hearing and eyesight and keenly aware of what is going on in their environment. If a turkey spots any kind of potential danger, it will sound the alarm note (a sharp cluck), if it has not already run or flown away. This makes killing a turkey of any age or sex in the fall (in states where the season is open) a trophy in my opinion, and the same holds true in the spring when only the mature toms (males two years of age or over) and jakes are legal. (In some states bearded hens are legal in the spring; check your home state's regulations.)

One of many marvelous aspects of turkey hunting is that we interact with these big game birds by calling to them. To learn how to call, we have to master how to make sounds with the three major calling devices: box calls, pot and pegs, and diaphragms. Box calls are the easiest to use, as all one has to learn how to do is slide the lid across the surface of the box in such a way as to produce turkey-like sounds.

Pot and pegs typically have a hollow circular pot with a surface of slate, aluminum, or glass. The peg, which is usually made of some sort of wood and is also called a striker, makes contact with the pot surface and sounds are produced. Of our trio, this type of call is generally the second easiest to learn how to manipulate

The diaphragm, or mouth call, consists of latex stretched across a horseshoe-shaped frame that is small enough to fit neatly inside our mouths. The huge advantage of using this call is that we don't have to use our hands in order for it to make sounds. This is important when the quarry is a turkey, which can spot even the smallest movement from many yards away. I spent many months of practice before I could manipulate my tongue and the diaphragm in just the right way.

With these call making devices, hunters can make yelps (yawk, yawk, yawk), clucks (chuck, chuck, chuck), cuts (high-pitched excited sounds), and many other of the two dozen sounds that turkeys utter. But if you can just learn how to simulate reasonably realistic clucks and yelps, you can call in turkeys.

The vast majority of turkey hunters employ 12 gauge shotguns with full chokes; full chokes constrict the pattern of the pellets after they pass through the barrel. Most hunters strive to hunt turkeys when they are within 40 yards or closer, so most of the time hunters pattern their guns to shoot accurately at 30 to 40 yards. The best way to kill a turkey is to aim at the base of the neck, so that the pattern of pellets saturates the head and neck area. Hunters often debate whether No. 4, 5, or 6 shot is best for accomplishing this. With my 12 gauge Remington 1100 autoloader, size 4 shots perform the best.

Another major point involves how to set up on a turkey. In both the spring and the fall, you are trying to call the turkey to your stationary position. I like to be positioned so that when the turkey first comes into view, it is within 40 yards. Turkeys expect to see the "bird" that has been calling to them, and if they do not, they often quickly become very suspicious/fearful and will flee.

And when that turkey does appear at, say, 40 yards, don't move to shoot at it until its head disappears behind some obstacle such as a tree. If you try to slowly raise your shotgun or even quickly raise it, the turkey will see your actions and run or fly away. Some hunters use turkey decoys to help keep a turkey in the area; others feel that fake birds can alarm a turkey. I've been able to kill some turkeys only because a decoy was out some 20 yards in front of me, but I've also had turkeys come within 40 yards of my position, espy the decoy, and then turn around and run away.

Another important consideration is camouflage. In the fall, I wear patterns that feature the browns, oranges, and blacks of the autumn woods. Come spring, the color green will be predominant. During both seasons, I always don a camo face mask to further conceal the fact that I am a predator.

The last tidbits of advice are based on lessons it took me 15 years to learn and resulted in my blowing many opportunities for success during the interim. The first is, do not try to move a little closer to a turkey when it is already within 100 yards or so of you. Turkeys are on "turkey time." Once on their way to your position, chances are that they will continue to come, but they may also stop to feed, poop, preen, and look around for predators and other turkeys.

Author Bruce Ingram with a wild turkey he called in and killed. Turkeys are Bruce's favorite game animal to hunt.

Second, calling softly and infrequently is almost always better than calling loudly and often. The major exception is on a fall hunt when you have broken up (scattered) a flock of jakes and jennies (young females). The jennies will kee-kee (a panic stricken whistle-like sound, wee-wee-wee, wee-wee-wee; the males make the same wee-wee-wee sound but add yawp-yawp-yawp to it) and the jakes may produce a few adolescent gobbles. But both sexes are desperate to reunite with their flock members and will begin calling loud and often about 15 to 30 minutes after the bust. You should too.

And, third, once you know that birds are in the area and sit down and begin calling, don't move. I really, really mean that. Many times turkeys will come into your calls, say, an hour after you have begun calling and about 45 minutes later than you think they should have. Those birds, many times, will not have answered you at all, but have been slowly coming your way the entire time—remember they are on turkey time. Then when a turkey finally comes to your position, often from behind or to your side, it sees an idle hand scratch an itch. The next sound you will hear will be the alarm putt (a loud chuck) and then the flapping of wings.

Lastly, please consider joining the National Wild Turkey Federation. The NWTF is not only an organization for those who enjoy turkey hunting, but also a major, national conservation organization with state and local chapters across the country. The NWTF magazine contains many articles on conservation, habitat improvement projects, and of course turkey hunting. Those local chapters can be great places for a new hunter to find mentors and learn how to be an outdoorsman. I have been a proud member for over 30 years. Matt Lindler, editor of the NWTF magazine *Turkey Country*, says the organization stands ready to help novice youth and adult hunters.

First, says Matt, by joining the NWTF, new members will receive *Turkey Country*, which offers articles on all aspects of successful turkey hunting, including the selection of guns, loads, chokes, and calls to use. In my opinion, one of the most impressive things about the magazine is its emphasis on how to improve wildlife habitat (and the biological reasons for doing so) not only for turkeys but also for other game and non-game animals. For example, I wrote a story for the magazine on how as a land owner, I was improving habitat for the threatened songbird, the golden-winged warbler.

"Our local chapters are also great resources for new hunters," says Lindler. "New hunters can find mentors there and learn how to become a voice for conservation issues in the local area, plus become part of a social network of people who love the outdoors. A lot of the fundraising our local chapters do benefits wildlife habitat improvement projects right there in the area where members live."

Turkey hunting is the most addictive, challenging, entrancing thing I do in the outdoors. I had rather bring home an 8-pound jenny than a 150-pound buck. When Elaine and I would go to her high school reunions, she wouldn't dance with me, saying that I have no rhythm or style—which is definitely true. But my sweet wife loves seeing me "dancing on the sundeck" which I often do when I bring home a turkey to her. I just can't help celebrating after I kill a fall or spring bird.

4. Wild Turkey Recipes

Wild turkey leg soup is a great meal on a cold fall or winter day.

Turkey Leg Soup and Sourdough Bread

Want to try a different way to utilize the meat from wild turkey legs? Then consider making it the main ingredient in a soup and sourdough meal. They may not be a classic combo like macaroni and cheese or ham and eggs, but wild turkey leg soup and sourdough bread were made to go together.

When I first began to become successful as a turkey hunter (after a steep learning curve), I called my turkey hunting friends about what to do with the meat. Many roasted the entire bird, à la the domestic counterpart, but Elaine and I found the extremely lean meat of the wild version unsuited for oven cooking.

Some hunting buddies deep fried the whole bird, but as health food devotees—and wild game provides the healthiest kind of meat—we avoid fried foods. One friend even suggested tossing the legs, stating that they were too tough to do anything with—a recommendation we immediately rejected as a shameful waste of wild game.

Finally, after some experimentation, Elaine came upon the solution of grilling the breasts and turning the leg meat into the main ingredient of soup. And a few years later, she came upon the serendipitous pairing of wild turkey leg soup and homemade sourdough bread.

"Just as Bruce experienced a learning curve with hunting wild turkeys, I went through some trial and error experiences toward finding what I feel is the best way to create the soup," says Elaine. "A key change I hit upon was adding flour as a thickening agent, which gives the soup a heartier consistency. Here's the recipe I eventually devised."

Elaine's Wild Turkey Leg Soup

Ingredients

3	medium potatoes, peeled and cubed
1	turnip, peeled and cubed
2	carrots, peeled and diced
4	celery stalks, diced
	Other mixed vegetables as desired
2	cups cooked, diced turkey
2	quarts chicken or turkey broth
1	onion, chopped
6	Tbsp butter or margarine
6	Tbsp all-purpose flour
	Salt and pepper to taste

Directions

Place the diced potatoes, turnip, carrots, and celery in 2 quarts chicken or turkey broth. Bring to a boil. Reduce the heat and cook until vegetables are tender, about 20 minutes. Drain, reserving the liquid and setting the vegetables aside. In the same kettle melt the butter and sauté the onion until tender. Stir in flour. Gradually add 1½ cups of the reserved broth, stirring constantly until thickened. Gently stir in cooked vegetables and diced turkey. Add the remaining reserved liquid, a cup at a time, until the soup is the desired consistency. Peas, lima beans, corn, cabbage, or other vegetables on hand may be added as well. Yield: 8–10 servings.

Sourdough Bread

Although we like the "sourness" of sourdough bread, the wheat flour in this recipe still leaves a touch of this sourness yet also provides the health benefits of whole wheat. Quick tip—time the cooking of the soup and bread so that both finish at the same time. The hot, hearty soup served together with the still steaming bread (slathered with butter) is a visual and taste sensation.

Fern Hollow's Golden Honey Bread
(Courtesy of Soc Clay)

Makes 1 quart of basic batter. Allow to set overnight in a warm place. (You will need a package of Soc Clay's Sourdough Starter or your own starter; ordering directions follow.)

1	quart sourdough batter
2	cups milk
2	Tbsp butter or margarine
2	Tbsp salt
2	Tbsp sugar
¼	cup honey
¼	cup wheat germ
2	cups wheat flour
4	cups all-purpose flour
2	tsp baking soda

In a large mixing bowl, scald two cups milk. Add butter and honey and allow to cool. Add to 1-quart sourdough batter. Stir in wheat flour and wheat germ. Blend sugar, salt, and soda until smooth and sprinkle over top of dough, stirring in gently. Cover dough and set in warm spot for 30 minutes. Break down and add remaining flour until dough is too stiff to stir. Turn out on floured surface and knead for 8–10 minutes or until dough feels light and satiny to the touch. Separate into two equal portions, flour lightly, fold over, seal seams, and place in greased 9" × 5" × 2½" baking pans. Grease top of dough with oil or margarine, set in warm spot until double in bulk (about 1–1½ hours). Preheat oven to 400°F and bake bread for 20 minutes, reduce heat to 325°F and continue baking another 20 minutes or until bread shrinks from the side of the pan. Remove bread from oven and turn out onto rack or towel and butter tops. Makes two loaves.

(Interestingly, Soc Clay's sourdough starter originated in the Alaskan Gold Rush from 1899–1901. Clay lists a number of recipes in *Soc Clay's Mad Trapper Sourdough Baking* recipe book. One of our favorites is the recipe for Soc's Blueberry Muffins.)

Wild Turkey Leg Sloppy Joes

For years, our two favorite ways to prepare wild turkey legs have been to cook them as part of a soup or as ground burger. But one day when we were dining on venison sloppy joes, made from ground meat from the front shoulders, we experienced an epiphany. Why had we never considered preparing Wild Turkey Leg Sloppy Joes?

Our error was easily corrected, and we now have a third favorite way to prepare the legs. The neck meat also serves well as part of this entrée. We prefer a 10-inch cast iron skillet for this dish, but any utensil made for stovetop cooking can suffice.

Ingredients

1	lb ground turkey
2	Tbsp olive oil
½	green pepper, chopped
½	sweet onion, chopped
2	cloves garlic, minced
1	stalk celery, chopped
1	15-oz. can tomato sauce
2	Tbsp brown sugar
2	tsp apple cider vinegar
1	tsp balsamic vinegar
1	Tbsp Worcestershire sauce
1–2	Tbsp yellow mustard
½	tsp smoked paprika
	Salt and pepper to taste

Directions

In a cast-iron skillet add 1–2 Tbsp olive oil. Brown the ground turkey over medium heat, along with the green pepper, onion, celery, and garlic. When the turkey is thoroughly cooked, add the remaining ingredients and cook uncovered over low heat until the mixture thickens, perhaps about 30 minutes. Stir often. You may have to reduce the heat if the mixture begins to thicken too much. Serve over buns or bread.

Notes
- Sloppy Joe meals of any kind come by their name honestly. This is an entrée best prepared by someone who doesn't mind having part of it ending up on a shirt. For workaday lunches, bring the "sauce" to work in a container and add it to the bread right before dining. Doing so will prevent the bread from becoming soggy.
- Although we prefer whole wheat rolls or bread for this dish, white rolls work well and the mixture is equally good over rice or even on baked potatoes.
- A medium size turkey will probably have enough leg meat for five sandwiches. Add in the neck meat and a sixth one is possible.
- We've found the easiest way to remove the meat from the legs is right after a turkey is killed. Use a boning or other sharp knife—and a good deal of patience. Then grind the turkey in a meat grinder and freeze. Or better yet, cook for dinner that night.

Turkey Neck Salad

As I admired the Sullivan County, Tennessee mature gobbler that my turkey hunting mentor, Elizabethton's Larry Proffitt, had just called in for me, I began thinking about the breasts my wife Elaine would grill and the legs she would turn into soup. But then I had another thought—what other parts of a turkey can be eaten?

"Surprisingly, the neck has a lot of good meat to it," said Proffitt after I put that thought into words. "I make turkey salad by cooking the meat off the bone in a pressure cooker. I bought a small food processor and put portions of the meat in it and grind it smooth as if I were making chicken salad. Add to the meat a cut up boiled egg, sweet pickle relish, and mayonnaise to taste. Turkey neck salad also makes great sandwiches."

Elaine and I don't care for pickle relish, so we experimented with Larry's recipe and made a few changes. We found that celery gives the dish a wonderful crunchy taste and helps hold the salad together.

Also, the first few times we had the dish it was the main course as a hearty salad, but then we decided to take Larry up on his suggestion to try turkey neck as the main ingredient in a sandwich. We found that several slices of sharp cheddar cheese, Romaine lettuce, and mustard slathered on two pieces of whole wheat bread really enhanced the sandwich.

Directions

In a small slow cooker, place one turkey neck and add water or chicken broth to almost cover. Cook on low for 6 hours, or until the meat can be easily pulled from the bone.

Allow to cool, then, using your fingers, separate meat from bones — this part is a little tedious, so take your time. Be careful to not let any of the small bones slip by. Also, be sure to carefully go through the meat and search for any shot pellets. Be careful to work your way thoroughly down between the neck bones to extract as much meat as possible, digging it out with your fingers or a fork when necessary.

Chop the meat with a cleaver or other knife. Larry's food processor, of course, works well for this, too.

To the meat, add 2 stalks chopped celery, ¼ cup chopped onion, 2 chopped hard boiled eggs, and ¼ cup mayonnaise. Stir well, adding salt and pepper to taste. This makes enough for 2 or 3 nice sandwiches or a hearty salad for two.

You can add optional, supplementary ingredients of your choosing—cranberries, grape halves, and chopped nuts are all tasty additions. In the fall, we like to add such wild nuts as black walnuts or shagbark hickory nuts that we have gathered. This, we believe, adds to the joy and experience of eating a wild turkey. In the spring, instead of onions, some folks like to use the native plant ramps. However, we feel the flavor of ramp overpowers that of the turkey neck—and everything else as well.

Summing Up

Nothing will ever change our opinion that dining on grilled turkey breast is the most sublime way to enjoy our favorite game animal. Although Turkey Neck Salad is a strange name for a menu item, it's a delightful taste experience, too. We like to combine this dish with some homemade bread, such as sourdough or traditional Southern cornbread, when dining at home. For workaday lunches, our choice is the salad as part of a sandwich for a very filling meal.

Turkey Neck Odds and Ends

Turkeys, of course, have very long necks, older toms especially. We prefer to hold the bird by the head, lay the neck on a cutting board, and use a knife to sever the neck where it adjoins the body. Then we use that same knife to detach the head.

If the neck is from a young fall bird, you may want to delay trying this recipe until you have tagged several turkeys. Neck meat is dark just like the leg version is, so if you are inclined, you can just add the neck meat to any recipe where you normally would use the legs (we prefer stew, soup, or pot pie)...or, conversely, use the legs for the salad recipe.

Of course, sometimes the neck will be so riddled with pellets that cooking it would be impractical. Then it's perfectly okay to just discard this part of a bird's anatomy.

5. Getting Started on Squirrel Hunting

When Kevin Boeren was 11, his father Bob brought the youngster over to my wife Elaine's and my rural Virginia property. The mission—to help Kevin kill his first squirrel. An hour or so later, the youngster employed a .22 to down his initial silvertail. Bob and I let out a whoop and Kevin sported a grin for the rest of the morning.

Regardless of whether someone is nine, 19, or 39, squirrels are a marvelous "starter" game animal, maintains Robert Abernethy, the National Wild Turkey Federation's assistant vice president of agency programs.

"Squirrels are abundant and found throughout the United States except for areas in the Great Plains where trees aren't available," he says. "They are especially important game animals in the Southeast, Northeast, and Midwest.

"They are also relatively easy to hunt, don't require an expensive rifle, just a .22 or a 20 gauge; and, very importantly, these new hunters can learn the basics of woodsmanship by pursuing squirrels."

To back up his statement on woodsmanship, Abernethy cites a West Virginia study where experienced deer, turkey, squirrel, and other categories of hunters were tested to see which groups knew the most about sign, tree identification, and in what kinds of habitat certain species of mast producers lived. The bushytail enthusiasts easily won.

Bob Boeren, a professional forester, agrees that the pursuit of squirrels is a wonderful way to teach woodsmanship.

"One of the best things about squirrels being the perfect starter game animal is that you don't have to be overly quiet when you're in the woods, so it's a great time to explain the basics of woodsmanship," he says. "On Kevin's early hunts, I took time out to show my son game trails and buck rubs and scrapes, what turkey scratching and droppings look like, and how to tell the differences between various white and red oak species and also several of the hickories.

"Kevin was curious about everything in the woods, even the moss and lichens. I really feel our time in the woods even has helped him do better in his school science classes."

Bob's comments on hickory nuts are quite relevant. One of the best squirrel hunters I know is Jerry Paitsel. He says that in early autumn, hickories (among them, one or more varieties thrive across the eastern half of the country) are the number one place to take a stand for silvertails. Jerry adds that two hunters can double team a squirrel that is feeding high in the treetops on hickories or other nuts, such as acorns.

In most states, squirrel seasons last from fall well into winter.

"A squirrel spotting one hunter will often shimmy around the tree, giving the second hunter a chance at a shot," he says. "Another solid tactic is to look for moving limbs, then look for the squirrel. I also prefer still hunting through the woods. By continuously moving, but moving slowly, I feel like that strategy will allow me to cover more ground and see more squirrels."

Finally, Jerry suggests that hunters listen for squirrels "barking." Squirrels don't bark like dogs, but they do make harsh, guttural "cuks" when they spot hunters or some other form of danger. Boeren believes that no magical age exists for when a child is ready to begin bagging bushytails.

"A lot depends on the maturity and interests of the child," the forester explains. "Kevin started by not carrying a gun, just tagging along on hunts. He was able to see me practice gun safety and wait for the right moment to take a shot.

"But I also made sure that he was very much an active participant in the hunt. If I were hunting squirrels, for example, Kevin was the one using a squirrel call to locate them. And while we were hunting squirrels, I let my son practice using deer grunt and bleat calls and various turkey calls. He also learned basic hunting strategies such as stand and still hunting. Again with squirrels, it's no big deal if a new hunter runs off a few of them."

The author with a squirrel he shot while hunting behind his house.
Squirrel populations are typically abundant throughout their range.

Like Abernethy, Boeren recommends that youngsters start squirrel hunting with smaller guns such as .22s and 20 gauges. The forester also suggests that when it's time to move on to deer rifles or shotguns for turkeys, that parents opt for youth models. I recommend hearing protection for sensitive young ears; this protection will also help prevent both youngsters and adults from flinching before a trigger is pulled.

Jerry Paitsel, who operates Struttinbird Turkey Calls, agrees about the use of a .22 rifle with a 2x to 7x scope as an excellent starter gun for kids and novice adults.

"When I was growing up, just about every kid in my neighborhood had a .22 single shot," he says. "Using that gun taught us so much about marksmanship, patience, and perseverance, as well as the need to make an accurate first shot so as not to spook the animal. A .22 also does less damage to the meat than a shotgun does with all its pellets."

For bullets, Jerry recommends a subsonic .22 long rifle hollow point, which does not make much sound (a quality all hunters of any age or experience level can appreciate) and also because it does not tear up much meat. Paitsel says hunters should aim for the head or right behind the front shoulder.

Jerry Paitsel is one of the best squirrel hunters that the author has ever gone afield with.

Boren further emphasizes that folks mentoring youth hunters should do all they can to make the outing a pleasurable one. He recommends the following items for a day pack.

- Snacks and water.
- Change of clothes in case the child becomes wet or cold.
- Mammal, bird, and tree identification books. Bob favors the Audubon series.
- Seat cushion.

"Kevin and I also have a tradition of going out to lunch after a morning hunt for any game animal," Boeren says. "This is something we both really look forward to so that we can relive the hunt and have quality time together."

Squirrels are perhaps the best game animal for
youngsters or novice hunters to pursue.

One last point concerning squirrel hunting that both Abernethy and Boeren agree on is that it is important for the novice adult hunter or child to share the day's bounty with other family members.

6. Getting Started on Rabbit and Grouse Hunting

Most rabbit hunters use beagles, but hunters can also still hunt bunnies.

By far, squirrels are the easiest small game animal to hunt, as well as the most abundant game animal in America. Rabbits and grouse also have their fans, but novice hunters should know that bunnies and fool hens, especially the latter, are much more difficult to hunt.

The cottontail rabbit typically lives in transitional habitat, that is, land that is in the process of changing from one type of habitat to another. For example, a great place to locate rabbits is a former agricultural field that has not been farmed for five to 10 years. Briers, brambles, berry vines, and small trees will have sprung up and created a tangled mess.

Another bunny hotspot is a clear cut that is five to ten years in age. If, as likely, the logger left piles of woody debris about, this type of habitat will host even more rabbits. This second growth, just like the overgrown fields, gives rabbits protection from winged and four-legged predators and abundant places to feed and breed.

Most people who pursue rabbits go afield with beagles. The bawling of the beagles, their chasing of the cottontails, and the comradery that exists on such a rabbit hunt is a delightful experience. Another thing I like about these affairs is that the participants generally divide up the game killed afterwards. As someone who has notoriously slow reflexes (rabbits make darting, daring runs and are difficult to hit), I really enjoy this aspect as all too frequently I'm the only one who has failed to down a bunny.

Many rabbit enthusiasts prefer a 20-gauge shotgun fueled with No. 5 or 6 shot. The higher the shot number, the more pellets there are and they are smaller, too. Many folks also prefer an improved cylinder choke (which is more open—that is, makes a more expansive pattern of pellets—than the tighter full and medium chokes). The wide pattern and the numerous pellets make it much easier to kill a bounding bunny.

Folks who don't know anyone with rabbit dogs, still can pursue cottontails. On early morning or late evenings in January and February, I like to slowly walk the edges of clear cuts and old fields and "jump shoot" any rabbits that I startle. My success rate is low—again that reflex problem—but this is a delightful way to begin or end a winter day.

Ruffed grouse are another important small game animal, and good friend Jay Honse is one of the best upland bird hunters I've ever had the pleasure to go afield with.

"Grouse typically live in 10- to 20-year-old second growth forests that are growing back from a clear cut," he says. "You can also find them in creek bottoms with lots of vegetation such as rhododendron and saplings and in mountain thickets with grape vines, mountain laurel, and lots of shrubby growth.

"Grouse are often much more abundant in the mountains of the North and Northeast than they are in the mountains of the Southeast. Hunters everywhere typically use pointing dogs like Brittany spaniels and English setters that will lock in [stand still with noses pointed and tails erect toward the hunkering grouse] on a grouse. When the grouse flushes, it comes up quickly and erratically, making it extremely difficult to hit. That they prefer thick cover just adds to the challenge of bringing one home."

Indeed, continues Jay, it is often an "event" to bring home a ruff. Jay says some individuals will use flushing dogs to pursue grouse; he, for example, is training Daisy, his yellow lab, to do just that. Hunters will closely follow a flushing dog and hope that they can squeeze off a shot before the dislodged ruff flies out of range.

Some hunters prefer the same shotguns, chokes, and loads that they do for rabbits. Jay, however, likes to use scatterguns with shorter barrels (22 to 24 inches) because of the tight, thick terrain that grouse prefer. He also prefers over/under shotguns, which have barrels arranged just like the name indicates. Good choke selections would be improved cylinder and cylinder, both of which present a wide pattern. The Virginian recommends No. 7 ½ shot.

Just as I do for rabbits, I like to still hunt for grouse on mid-winter days. And I am about as successful for the former species as I am the latter, which means I rarely bring one home.

"People grouse hunt for the experience," says Jay, "the joy of being outdoors and walking through the woods with their dog. This pastime is not about the killing."

7. Small Game Recipes

Here are Jerry Paitsel's directions for cleaning squirrels.

You'll need a small 3- or 4-inch fixed blade knife with a straight blade, game shears, and a large bowl to deposit the cleaned squirrels.

Holding the squirrel by its hind legs, cut through the anal area directly under the tail. Next, cut away a little of the skin under the hind quarters. Then, stand on the tail and holding onto both hind legs, pull upward until the hide slides off the lower body and all the way to the neck and front paws.

A strip of skin will remain under the stomach; cut this off. Next, use the game shears to cut off the front paws, the back paws, and head.

Then open the chest cavity from the anal area up to the rib cage and remove the entrails. Using the game shears, cut off the rib cage. Cut off the front and back legs and put them in the bowl. All that is left now is the back meat, which is high quality, emphasizes Jerry. Put that part in the bowl, too.

Here are Jay Honse's directions for cleaning rabbits and grouse.
- For rabbits, be sure to wear rubber gloves because some animals have been infected with tularemia, a rare infectious disease. To avoid this affliction, cook rabbit meat at least to 170°F.
- Remove the entrails by opening up the anal area and pulling them out.
- Then pull the back skin of the rabbit upward, make a slit and slowly pull the hide off (with both hands and in opposite directions). Use game shears to snip off the paws and head.

You can cook the rabbit whole or snip off the legs and back and cook just those parts.

For grouse, Jay follows this procedure:
- Cut off the head, wings, tail, and feet with game shears.
- Remove the entrails by opening up the anal area and pulling them out.
- Pluck some feathers from breast area, insert knife below the breast; with both hands pull skin away from breast area and toward and over extremities.
- Cut off the legs and breast and prepare for cooking.

Jerry Paitsel's Simple Squirrel Stew

Ingredients

Two or three squirrels	
Can of chicken broth	
Favorite vegetables: onions, potatoes, peas, lima beans, and celery for example.	

Directions

Put all of the ingredients in a slow cooker and simmer on medium for six hours or until the meat has fallen from the bone and is quite tender.

Elaine's Baked Squirrel Casserole

Ingredients

	Squirrels, skinned and cleaned for cooking
1	can condensed cream of mushroom or cream of celery soup
1	onion, roughly chopped
2–3	carrots, cubed
1–2	potatoes, sliced

Directions

Place the squirrel parts in a casserole dish that has a lid. Lay the vegetables over top of the squirrel pieces.

Dilute the soup with about ½ can of water. Pour over the meat and vegetables. Place the lid on the casserole dish and put into oven.

Bake at 350°F for 1 ½ to 2 hours

Jim Crumley's Easy Does It Recipe for Squirrels and Rabbits

Ingredients

Squirrels and/or rabbits	
Chicken broth	
Canola oil	

Directions

Cut squirrel and or rabbit meat into serving size pieces. Put in aluminum foil with a little chicken broth.

Wrap and put in slow cooker on low for 6 hours, or until meat is almost falling from bone. Let cool, then dredge through seasoned flour.

Brown quickly in frying pan in canola oil, let drain on paper towels or in low heat oven, and serve. If in a hurry, pressure cooker can be used for the first cooking phase.

Betty Honse's Grouse with Apple Slices

Before cooking grouse that her husband Jay has brought home, Betty recommends soaking them overnight or at least several hours in a brine made of 2 cups apple juice, 2 tablespoons salt, and 2 tablespoons sugar. This helps tenderize and keep the birds moist.

Ingredients

2	grouse
2	peeled sliced apples
	Salt and pepper
¼	cup apple juice

Directions

Pat birds dry. Season with salt and pepper. Rub breasts with softened butter. Place pieces of apple under birds, in cavity and on top of breast secured with toothpick.

Pour ¼ cup apple juice over birds before covering with foil. Place in small baking dish covered with foil or wrap individually.

Bake at 350°F for approximately 1 hour. After opening foil, birds may be basted with butter and returned to oven for 15 minutes to brown.

II. Getting Started on Freshwater Fishing

Across the country, members of the black bass and sunfish families are found just about everywhere in one or more of the four major habitat types: lakes, ponds, rivers, and creeks. The black bass and sunfish family members thrive in what are known as warm water environs, while members of the trout family fall under the cold water classification. Other popular game fish include walleyes, muskies, crappie, and catfish (channel, flathead, and blue).

The natural progression of many people is to begin fishing with worms or night crawlers as children, switch to live minnows as they grow a little older, and then as older teenagers or adults turn to spinning and baitcasting rods and reels and/or to fly rods. When fishing for trout, I rarely use anything but a fly rod, while going after bass and sunfish, I employ spinning rods, baitcasters, and fly rods—depending on the season or the situation.

For example, if I am fishing for lake largemouths in winter, I will typically use a baitcaster rod with slow, bottom bumping baits such as a tube, as the fish are typically lethargic and holding close to the bottom. If I am after river smallmouths on a hot, sunny summer afternoon, I may drift lazily along and cast fly rod poppers to shade pockets along the shoreline. If it is springtime and I'm on a river and the bass are actively chasing, say, minnows, I might use a spinning rod and a fly rod and cast, respectively, a hard plastic minnow bait and a streamer (a minnow imitating fly).

My point is that I am not a purist, preferring to use the rods, lures, and flies that the season dictates. Baitcasters have reels that have to spin to release line. Because of this (I guess it must be some law of physics) these reels do not cast light (typically less than ⅜-ounce lures) well. If you use lighter lures (or even heavy ones) on a baitcaster, do not be surprised if you get a backlash (a tangled mess of line). Baitcaster rods are stout affairs and made to subdue big fish. I would not recommend beginning to fish with a baitcaster.

Spinning outfits make excellent beginning and expert outfits. The spinning reel is stationary but has a revolving medal "arm" that clasps the line and feeds it onto the reel as you turn the reel handle. When you want to cast, flip the arm and tuck the now disengaged line under an index finger pressed close to the rod. Cock the rod over a shoulder and quickly bring the rod and your arm forward and pointing in the direction you want the lure to travel, meanwhile and simultaneously releasing the line with your finger. Don't be discouraged if this casting process takes practice. Soon, though, muscle memory will come into play and you will begin to cast accurately.

Fly rods are often longer and springier than their baitcaster and spinning counterparts. With a spinning outfit, for example, the weight of the artificial helps propel itself as the line leaves the reel. With a fly rod, the weight of the line carries the fly to its destination. While working on this book, I received a 48-page booklet covering the basics of fly fishing. Similar length tomes would be needed to cover the elementals of using spinning and baitcasting outfits.

My best advice would be to start your fishing career with a medium action 6-foot spinning outfit, spooled with 8-pound-test monofilament line. (For spinning and baitcast rods, the lower the number the lighter the line and the easier it will break; 8-pound test is a medium light line.) Use that outfit, and the following lures (and tactics) for a season or two and then begin to branch out to other rods, lures, flies, and strategies.

For lure choices, I asked friend and fishing guide Richard Furman, who is one of the best all-around fishermen I have ever met, to suggest lures that would entice just about any game fish that fins fresh water.

"A 1/8-ounce Roostertail spinner will catch any species of black bass, sunfish, trout, or crappie," he says. "The flashing blade of this spinner [all spinners have blades that rotate around the body of the lure] and the feather-like hackle around the treble hook are very attractive."

Like Richard, my first choice for an all-species lure is a spinner, in this case a Size 2 Mepps Aglia. It is the ideal beginner lure and works great on a medium action spinning outfit. I've caught bass, trout, and sunfish on this blade bait. Merely cast the lure outward and begin retrieving it at a moderate pace as soon as it enters the water. You'll catch fish.

"My second choice would be a 2-inch, silver Rapala Original floating diving minnow," continues Richard. "With this lure, you can catch sunfish in a creek, smallmouths in a river, and largemouth bass and maybe even stripers in a lake. Moving through the water, this lure just looks like a sickly, struggling minnow which is often what triggers game fish to hit."

I share Richard's enthusiasm for the Rapala Original, believing that because of its fish attracting side to side wobble and its silver sides, it is one of the most effective artificials in the history of angling. Furman's next choice is also a favorite of mine.

"You have to have a crankbait [hard plastic lures that run under the surface when you crank the rod handle] in your game fish lineup and the Cordell Little O is one of the best all time," he says.

The Little O, like any crankbait, can be retrieved fast when the fish are active and slow when they are lethargic, and in-between when you want to give the fish a different look.

Richard's fourth and fifth picks are a 2 ½-inch tube (a short hollow soft plastic lure that has plastic strands dangling down) and a 5-inch slender finesse [meaning it is light and narrow in composition] plastic worm.

"Tubes imitate crayfish in the way they move through the water, and worms, well, imitate worms," says Richard. "I've caught huge bluegills from farm ponds on these baits, and I've caught big largemouths and smallmouths from rivers and lakes on them, too. Crappie will hit them, too."

Friend Paul Hinlicky with a fine smallmouth bass
caught on a float trip with Bruce.

Veteran angler Herschel Finch, who is the conservation columnist for the Potomac River Smallmouth Club's publication, *The Buzz*, agrees with Furman's choices.

"The Rooster Tails, Mepps, or Blue Fox inline spinners are perfect for beginners," he says. "Small, easy to fish and they will catch fish on them. The fish may not be large to start with, but early success is the key to getting an angler hooked on fishing. People can start branching out with surface baits and suspending jerkbaits [sinking, hard plastic baits imitating minnows] later when they get more accurate with their casting.

"As for baitcasting reels, I didn't pick up my first bait-casting rod until I was in my late 40s. Friend Al Pugh was my first instructor with them and he did a great job. Baitcasters are my main setup for casting jerkbaits, crankbaits, spinnerbaits, heavy jigs, and topwater baits. But I still like a good spinning rod for soft plastic baits, tubes, and light jigs [under ⅜ ounces] on the bottom."

One of the best all-purpose knots is the improved clinch, which can be used to tie line to a spool, or a lure, fly, or hook to the line. To begin, put about 4 inches of the end of the line through the eye of the lure or hook. Then wrap those 4 inches of line around the standing line five or six times, leaving a small loop near the hook eye. Next pass the end through the loop near the hook eye. Finally, pass the end through the last wrap on the other end, moisten the entire affair with saliva and draw tight. You may want to clip off a little bit of the tag end of the line, but don't cut so close that you threaten the integrity of the knot.

Regardless of whether a gamefish is finning about in a pond, stream, or impoundment, certain types of habitats will draw them. And these are the places you should cast to.

"Aquatic vegetation will often have some sort of game fish located nearby, as will rocks and wood," says Richard. "Fish like cover and those are the three main types. Fish, especially bigger ones, like a change in the bottom structure. For example, a drop-off of a foot or so in a mountain creek is likely to attract trout. A drop-off of a foot or two in a river with current is going to draw smallmouths and catfish. And a drop-off on the main channel of a lake is good place to look for largemouth bass, crappie, and bluegills."

I began my angling career as a wade fishermen in creeks, learning eventually to slowly slide my feet up and over rocks and wood, so as not to fall or make noise. Fish can easily detect intrusive underwater sounds. The only boat I have ever owned is a canoe which has served me well on rivers, creeks, and ponds. For these type of environs, many people also like kayaks which are cheaper and lighter than canoes. Motorized boats costing many thousands of dollars are often the choice of lake fishermen. For beginning fishermen, the financially sound choice is to wade fish local creeks and fish from the banks of nearby ponds and lakes to start. Then one day you can choose to buy the type of boat that best suits your angling style.

Part of the joy of fishing is exploring beautiful outdoor settings.

Three other relevant points need to be made, and, unfortunately, you will see many anglers not paying attention to any of them. First, any time you are wading or boating, you should have a lifejacket on. I always wear one while doing so and insist that anyone in my canoe have one on. Almost always when we read about someone drowning, two factors are mentioned: the person wasn't wearing a lifejacket and had imbibed alcohol.

Second, the warm weather period is when most people fish most often, myself included. No matter how hot the weather is, I always wear a long-sleeved nylon/polyester shirt and a pair of nylon/polyester pants, plus a hat. Nylon and polyester quickly dry when I become wet or perspire and the long sleeves and pants help protect me from sunburn.

Third, always try to go fishing with a friend. It's so much more pleasurable to do, to commiserate with when the action is slow, and to celebrate with when the bite is strong. But it's also a good idea to have someone along in case some mishap occurs. Fishing is truly a sport of a lifetime and a hobby that can be started at any stage of our lives.

How to Fillet a Fish

Filleting is the easiest way to prepare fish for cooking.

First, place the fish on a non-slip surface such as a cutting board

Using a fillet knife, make an incision behind the gills and downward to the backbone where the bones are.

Slide the knife along the backbone all the way to the tail.

Flip the skin over so that the skin is now touching the cutting board.

Slide the knife along next to the skin all the way to the other side of the fish.

You now have a boneless slice of healthy meat.

Repeat this process on the other side of the fish.

Please remember to never cut toward the hand that is holding the fish.

8. How to Fish for Bass

Black bass (largemouth, smallmouth, and spotted are the three major species) live in every state in the country except Alaska. Although walleyes are the most popular gamefish locally in some Midwestern states and trout can make the same claim in some Northeastern and Northwestern areas, overall, black bass are the most sought after gamefish in America.

I am not immune to their charms, as the smallmouth bass is my favorite fish to pursue, and the subject of my first five books. Paddling down a river and fishing for smallmouths is my favorite summertime activity, and this species, like other black bass, can be pursued throughout the entire year. However, especially in northern climes, catching bass is much more difficult come winter as they are cold-blooded creatures that often become quite lethargic when water temperatures dip below 40 to 45 degrees. Britt Stoudenmire, who operates the New River Outdoor Company, gives this year-round game plan.

"I utilize the jig and pig [jigs are hair or synthetic material tied around a hook; pigs are soft plastic baits that look like crayfish and are attached to the jig] during the cold water periods when water temps are typically 45 degrees and below. I impart a drag and stop presentation, often letting the jig sit for long periods before repeating the presentation again.

"I lean towards a suspending jerkbait [hard plastic minnow imitation] in the spring and fall when water temps are either rising or falling around the 50-degree mark. I like to rip [reel quickly with hard jerks] and then pause the jerkbait. Bass will often attack the bait and miss it, so it's paramount to keep working the lure until the fish eats it."

Britt says crankbaits work well any time of year when the water is slightly to heavily stained. The key to effectively fishing a crankbait is to make sure that the bait is in touch with the bottom, thus bouncing off all cover including rocks and wood. "I do not have as much success with these baits when they are not in contact with the bottom," he says.

Come summer, the guide switches to soft plastic baits.

"Mizmo tubes [crayfish imitating baits] and Yamamoto Senkos [minnow imitations] are a go to in the warm months with the water is low and clear. I make log casts and slowly retrieve these baits."

Summer is when bass most often rise to the surface to smash lures.

"I like to fish various topwaters in the warm months but prefer the buzzbait [a lure that churns across the surface like an eggbeater] over all others when the conditions are right like an overcast day. A buzzbait can cover a lot of water and simply attracts big fish. Make sure to get the bait turning after it hits the water and reel it just fast enough to keep it on the surface."

Britt says on rivers and creeks, bass prefer to be near current and anywhere a break, a depth decrease, occurs. Of course, both current and breaks are more likely to hold bass if rock, wood, or vegetation exists as well. In lakes and ponds, the current, such as it is, is not as big a factor, but bass are still likely to be found near cover and where depth changes exist.

For more information: www.newriveroutdoorco.com.

On rivers and lakes, most anglers today catch and release their black bass, as these waters often sustain heavy fishing pressure, and bass populations would decline if everyone kept their fish. The best place to go to catch bass to eat are ponds, where the fish of all species will often overpopulate this body of water if some are not kept.

Brett Stoudenmire is an expert bass fisherman and has
the knowledge to catch fish throughout the year.

9. How to Fish for Trout

One of the most gifted trout guides I know is Josh Williams, who operates Dead Drift Outfitters (www.deaddriftva.com). He suggests that beginning anglers who want to catch fish to take home visit their local put-and-take trout fisheries. Put-and-take waters are those streams and lakes stocked with trout that come from hatcheries—fish, in other words, that are raised to be caught and have little chance of ever becoming truly wild and reproducing. Often the bodies of water that these trout are stocked in can't support fish during the summertime because their water becomes too low and hot—again another reason for folks to take these fish home for a meal.

"When you come to a put-and-take stream or any kind of trout water, take a few minutes and study the stream before you cast," says Josh. "Put on a pair of polarized sunglasses and look at the various features of the stream. Chances are that you'll see the four major forms of trout water.

"Somewhere up ahead of you [and you should always wade upstream when trout fishing because doing so makes it less likely you'll alarm fish] you'll see a stretch of riffles [swift water with a *chop* to it], an undercut bank that has deeper, darker water and is a good place for trout to ambush food drifting downstream, and mid-stream rocks, which have little eddies or slack water behind them. Trout will hold in the slack water because they don't have to expend much energy to do so, then dart out to the sides of the rock to eat food that is drifting by."

The fourth type of trout holding area is a plunge pool, perhaps the most beautiful place on a trout stream. Plunge pools are formed by small waterfalls; the falling of the water hollows out the stream below, often making plunge pools the home of the deepest water on any trout stream, says Josh. Worms, minnows, salmon eggs, and spinners are four solid choices to entice put-and-take trout. Fished on a medium or light action spinning rod, this quartet will produce.

After a few years of fishing put-and-take streams, anglers may want the challenge of fishing wild trout streams (streams where the fish reproduce on their own or are supplemented by the stocking of small trout, called fingerlings, that become wild). Another worthy quarry is the native brook trout which dwells in mountain streams throughout the Appalachian mountain chain.

"For wild and native trout, I recommend catching and releasing them," says Williams. "They are too valuable and uncommon a resource to be caught just once and kept. I like to think that the trout I release, someone else or myself will catch them or their offspring some year in the future. On these streams, many anglers use a fly rod, and on some of these waters only fly rods are permitted by the fishing regulations."

Regarding fly rods for these type streams (remember that with this type of rod the line provides the weight to cast a fly), Williams suggests a 6 ½ to 7-foot long, 4-weight one (the lower the number the lighter, less substantial, the rod is; rods for big bass are often 9 or 10 weight and are designed for casting heavy fly patterns). Josh pairs this rod with a 12-foot, 5x leader.

A leader is a tapered line that is at its narrowest where the fly is attached. The lower the leader X number is, the more substantial and heavier it is. A leader that is 5x in size is good for casting Size 14 to 20 fly patterns. On wild and native streams, Josh says these flies should mimic creatures such as mayflies, caddis, and stoneflies.

Two other gear items you'll likely want to purchase are wading shoes (which have specially designed soles that help "grip" the stream bottom) and a landing net. Many anglers today prefer nets made from rubber as they are less abrasive to a fish's delicate body. River smallmouth fishing is my favorite type of fishing activity, but I also delight in visiting wild and native trout streams. You may well feel the same way one day.

Guide Josh Williams playing a trout on a mountain river.

10. How to Fish for Panfish

Panfish include two main fish families. The sunfish, which include both black and white crappie as well as redbreast sunfish, rock bass, pumpkinseed, shellcracker, and many more; and perch, which include the walleye, sauger, and both yellow and white perch. Unless a lake, river, or other body of water is almost devoid of fish, no one need feel guilty about bringing panfish home to eat. If their numbers are not reduced in many of their habitats, they tend to reproduce to such a degree that the fish end up being stunted. This is especially true of white crappie in ponds and bluegills in lakes.

Some panfish prefer moving water or at least some water with current; for example, the rock bass and redbreast sunfish are often found in upland rivers, and black crappie do well in tidal streams. Others, such as bluegills and shellcrackers, thrive in still water environs.

Crappie are a great tasting fish, as are other panfish such as bluegills, rock bass, and yellow perch just to name a few.

Like any game fish, panfish relate or hold near cover. Rock bass, as their name suggests, typically thrive in flowing water with rocky bottoms. Redbreast sunfish often do well in rivers, too, but prefer the calm water below the rocky riffles. In other words, their habitat begins where that of the rock bass ends. Bluegills relish hunkering down near a stump or dock in a pond or lake.

Except for the walleye which can grow quite large, most panfish are between five and ten inches. If you catch a rock bass, redbreast, bluegill, or shellcracker that is 10 inches or more in length, that is a very fine fish. And catching these fish is generally not very hard except in the wintertime.

Something as simple as a worm impaled on a hook beneath a bobber will catch all manners of panfish. A small spinner or ultralight crankbait will fetch fish, too. And for sheer fun, few things are more pleasurable than catching panfish by using a fly rod and a Size 10 popping bug.

If you're planning on taking home a "mess" for dinner, bring along an ice chest and a large, clear plastic bag. As you catch fish, place them in the bag, and make sure to re-cover the top of the chest. As soon as fishing is over for the outing, fillet the fish (see the sidebar in Chapter II) and place them back in the bag and cover it with ice. The colder you keep the fish, the better they will taste. Never, never put your fish on a stringer in lake or river water. The fish will quickly die, and bacteria will just as quickly begin to perform their loathsome work.

Favorite Fish to Eat

If I had to list my five favorite fish to eat, they would be, in order, stripers, walleyes, channel catfish, black crappie, and rainbow trout. Rock bass, white crappie, bluegills, yellow perch, and blue catfish rank highly as well.

11. Fish Recipes

Friends Richard and Sandy Furman shared these recipes from their respective mothers.

Dot Furman's Barbecued Bass or Sunfish

Ingredients

2	lbs of fillets
½	cup of cooking oil
¼	cup sesame seeds
⅓	cup of lemon juice
⅓	cup cognac
3	tablespoons soy sauce
1	tsp salt
1	clove of garlic, crushed

Directions

Place fillets in a single layer in shallow bowl. Combine other ingredients and pour over fish. Let stand 30 minutes, turning once.

Remove fish, and reserve sauce for basting. Place fish on well-greased wire grills. Cook 8 minutes on barbecue grill about 4 inches from moderately hot coals.

Baste while fish is cooking. Turn and cook about 7 minutes on other side. Serve remaining sauce with fish. Makes 6 servings

Helen Riddle's Fried Fish

Ingredients

2 to 4	lbs of fish fillets (usually in large chunks)
1	bag of herb seasoned stuffing (example, Pepperidge Farms Herb Seasoned Stuffing)
	Vegetable oil (enough to come up to the sides of the fish, but don't cover fish entirely)
1	cup all-purpose flour (for coating fish)
½	cup of milk (or enough for dipping fish)
2	well-beaten eggs
	Salt and pepper to taste

Directions

Dip clean dry fish in milk. Roll fish in plain all-purpose flour, then dip in well beaten eggs. Roll in herb seasoned crushed stuffing crumbs, and fry in hot oil 375°F for 3 to 4 minutes per side, being careful not to burn the fish.

Dot Furman's Baked Stripers

Ingredients

2 to 4	lbs of striper fillets
	Diced tomatoes, chopped fine
1	can of tomato paste
	Chopped onions and peppers
	Garlic salt and pepper

Directions

Put striper fillets in aluminum foil and seal
Bake about 30 minutes at 325°F or until fillets are about ⅔ done
Open up foil and spread tomato bits and tomato paste on top of fillets
Sprinkle garlic salt and pepper and close foil
Bake another 10 to 15 minutes at 325°F
Note: great as a hot meal or a cold workaday lunch in foil

Our grandson Eli eating catfish chowder. The catfish
clan are among the best tasting gamefish.

Elaine and Sarah's Cheesy Catfish Chowder

Ingredients

2	Tbsp olive oil
1	Tbsp butter
½	cup chopped onions
1	cup chopped celery
1	cup chopped carrot
1	large white potato, peeled and cubed
2½	cups chicken broth
½	tsp dried thyme
½	tsp sea salt
¼	tsp ground pepper
¼	cup half and half
1 to 1¼	lb catfish, cut into chunks
1½	cups grated cheddar cheese

Directions

In a large stockpot, melt the butter with the olive oil. Sauté the onions until tender, about 5 minutes. Add the carrots, celery, potato, broth, and thyme. Simmer gently until the vegetables are tender, about 10–12 minutes.

Add the catfish chunks to the broth mixture and cook until done, about 5 minutes. Once the fish has turned white and is cooked through, add the half and half. Remove the pot from the heat and add the cheese to the soup, allowing it to melt gently.

Makes 4 servings.

Enjoy!

Belizean Fish Pouches

Good friend Lee Stoudenmire, who operates the New River Outdoor Company along with her husband Britt, shares with readers one of her favorite fish entrées.

"While we were traveling in Belize, we had a traditional Belizean dish several times that we loved," she says. "We had it in fancy restaurants as well as on beach barbecues when on snorkeling trips. After our second trip there, I began tweaking ingredients and finally found a good mix of ingredients that were both easy to find at home but also kept with the traditional Belizean dish. I also began using freshwater fish we could find here in the states, and they taste just as good in the recipe. It's also a great way to use up veggies from the fridge or garden."

Britt adds that his three favorite freshwater fish to eat are yellow perch, walleye, and rainbow trout and all are worthy candidates for this entrée.

Ingredients

4	fillets of your favorite fish (We've used several different panfish such as crappie, sunfish, and perch. I can't imagine any type of fish not turning out great.)
2	potatoes (any variety), diced into small cubes
1	green, yellow or red sweet bell pepper (or a mix thereof), sliced into strips
1	yellow onion, sliced into rounds, then halved

	Tomatoes (I like to use sweet garden varieties such as grape or cherry), halved
4	cloves garlic, peeled and crushed to release juices
	(Optional) Other veggies — asparagus, green beans, squash, zucchini, sugar snap peas, anything to clean out the fridge or use up from the garden, cut into strips (if applicable).
	Juice of 1 lime (or lemon if that's what you have)
	Hand full of cilantro, chopped (optional)
1	Tbsp butter, divided
	Extra virgin olive oil
	Salt and pepper to taste
	Hot sauce, to taste

Directions

Tear off four pieces of heavy duty aluminum foil (wide sheets if you have it, if not, double up).

Tear off four pieces of parchment paper; lay each sheet of parchment on top of 1 sheet of foil. (Easiest if you have the counter space to spread them all out and assemble pouches in an assembly-line manner.)

First drizzle ¼ teaspoon extra virgin olive oil on parchment

Lay fillet on oil and rub around to spread out the oil a bit

Salt and pepper lightly

On top of fish, add 1 crushed clove of garlic, bell pepper strips, potatoes, onion, tomatoes, and other veggies (optional).

Add a few sprigs of cilantro, to taste

Add a small dollop of butter on top

Sprinkle the pile with salt & pepper to taste (You could also use another herb-blend of seasoning here. Lemon pepper is great)

Dot hot sauce, to taste.

Squeeze lime (or lemon) juice on top.

It's nice to have an extra set of hands while folding the pouches but you can do it solo. They don't have to be perfect. Carefully pull parchment up from the sides and fold on top into a sealed pouch. While holding your parchment pouch with one hand, pull foil up and around parchment pouch, making sure to leave room around the pile of fish in sort of a "dome." Make sure to seal all edges of the foil well. You do not want any of the steam to escape from the pouch. It's okay if the parchment comes loose a bit as you fold the foil, as long as the foil is sealed properly. The parchment is there as a non-stick barrier between the fish and foil.

Place pouches directly on a hot grill and allow to cook for 20–30 minutes, depending on thickness of fish fillets and potatoes. Do not peak inside the pouches. This is tempting but will hinder the cooking process. You may also choose to cook the pouches in the oven at 450°F for 20–30 minutes.

Carefully remove foil pouch (I use tongs and grab the thick seam at the top) and let it cool for a few minutes before opening.

Be very careful when opening the pouches, the hot steam will burn you.

Serve with black beans and rice (a traditional Belizean side dish, recipe included also).

Belizean Black Beans and Rice

Ingredients

1	cup Jasmine rice
¾	cup coconut milk
¾	cup water
1	can black beans, drained not rinsed
	Salt, to taste

Directions

Combine coconut milk, water, rice, and salt. Bring to a boil over medium heat. Lower heat, cover and cook for 15 minutes, stirring occasionally to ensure it doesn't scorch. At about the 15-minute mark, stir in beans. If liquid evaporates before rice is completely done, stir in more water (about ½ cup at a time) and cook until rice is tender.

III. Getting Started on Gathering Wild Fruits and Nuts

What could be better in life than walking through woods, edges, overgrown fields, or along rural roads and gathering wild fruits and nuts, listening to songbirds, identifying trees and wildlife, and experiencing refreshing exercise? And, by the way, knowing that these fruits and nuts are free and can be prepared in all manners of tasty desserts or toppings on everything from morning oatmeal and cereal to scrumptious desserts like pies and homemade breads.

People who observe me going a-gathering sometimes warn me about the danger of being bitten by a timber rattler or copperhead, the two venomous snakes that live in Southwest Virginia where I do. Actually, I have never encountered either of these reptiles in a berry thicket, although it is certainly possible to do so. I fish, hunt, and gather year-round, know how to identify these two reptiles, and know what kind of habitats they dwell in. Many years have passed since I have seen either one on my ramblings. Folks, please don't let an irrational fear of snakes, as well as lions, tigers, and elephants, keep you from becoming a gatherer.

What are real threats are ticks (especially the blacklegged tick that carries Lyme disease, LD) and mosquitoes (which can cause West Nile virus). As someone who is currently recovering from Lyme disease (I was bitten while walking across a cow pasture early one April), I am especially sensitive to the LD threat. When picking berries, Elaine and I always try to wear rubber boots and long pants (tucked inside the boots) and long sleeve shirts and a hat. I also liberally spray my clothes with insect repellent.

Upon arriving home, we immediately check each other for ticks, and then shower. All these precautions did not keep me from initially contracting LD, but they certainly decrease my chances of having another case or being bitten by mosquitoes. Knee-high rubber boots also offer some protection from snakes.

Finding and Picking Wild Berries

Berry thickets are one of the most beautiful sights in nature. On a summer morning, the ripe berries glisten from the dew and are easily spotted from afar. The summertime berries (the raspberry, blackberry, wineberry, and dewberry) prefer early successional areas, meaning they are one of the first plants to colonize a woodlot that has been clearcut or a field that has been abandoned. They also thrive along the edges of fields and forests. On our Botetourt County, Virginia land, one of our most expansive patches is the one that grows between a wildlife food plot and an oak grove zone. Most of our other patches grow at the edge of our woods. The fall fruits and nuts live in more restrictive habitats and will be described in their respective chapters.

Health Benefits

Wild fruits and nuts are among the most nutritious of all foods. For example, members of the *Rubus* family, such as the blackberry, raspberry, dewberry, and wineberry, offer flavonoids, anti-oxidants, and Vitamins C and K, among other charms. Basically, this means they offer protection against cancer, premature aging, and infections. Nuts are rich in vitamins, minerals, and anti-oxidants as well as the extremely important Omega-3 fatty acids, which are heart-healthy and help result in good cholesterol ratings and can even lessen joint pain.

All of these fruits and nuts are important wildlife foods, as well, and I have observed wild turkeys and songbirds nesting and feeding within summer berry patches.

In addition to protective clothing as described below, you will need only a quart container or two and a handy manual such as *A Field Guide to Trees and Shrubs* (published by Peterson).

12. Blackberries and Dewberries

Well over a hundred species and hybrids of wild blackberries exist, and they thrive over most of the eastern half of the country. In the summer, they are the major berry producer where I live, and that's true in most of their range, too. I have seen blackberry vines that approached seven feet in height but most are four to five feet and grow upright or as arches. Come spring, I also can locate new blackberry patches by noting the abundant white blooms that really stand out.

Wild blackberries thrive over much of the country
and are easy to identify as well.

The stems flaunt thorns. The compound palmated leaves (usually they grow in threes but sometimes fives in my area, and are three to five inches long) are prickly. During blackberry season, my fingers will have several splinters embedded and my thumbs especially will be purple colored—but these minor annoyances are well worth the temporary and inconsequential pain. The berries are, of course, black, very tart, and each berry consists of many small oval drupes.

The common dewberry is like a ground growing version of the blackberry. The leaflets and blooms are very similar to those of the blackberry, but the dewberry itself is much sweeter and not at all tart. I have never gathered more than a cup at a time, and those precious cups are to be much treasured. Usually, though we never gather enough dewberries to be more than just a complement to blackberries in whatever dessert we are making. The dewberry mostly grows in the Mid-Atlantic and Northeast.

13. Raspberries

By far, the raspberry is our favorite summer wild fruit. The purplish black berries are sweeter than those of the dewberry, the briars are not as fearsome as those of the blackberry, and the vines feature a beautiful bluish/white hue. On our land, the leaflets usually come in threes, though fives are also possible. Raspberries grow in the entire eastern half of the country and range as far west as Colorado.

Wild black raspberries are Bruce and Elaine's favorite wild berry because of the pleasing sweetness they possess.

Another interesting trait of raspberry is that the vines sometimes bend over and root. The only problem with the raspberry is that blackberry and wineberry vines often seem to outcompete it, so we never seem to be able to gather more than a pint, or a quart at most, in any given expedition. But my, oh my, what jewels those few berries are. Having a raspberry pie or cobbler on a snowy winter day is a joy in life to be treasured.

14. Wineberries

Introduced into the United States in the late 1800s and now thriving from eastern Canada to Georgia and westward to Michigan and Arkansas, the wineberry is an Asian invasive species that features many pros and cons. And that's why I gave more space to it than the other summer fruits—matters are complicated with the wineberry. When we think of non-native flora and fauna, we often consider the numerous species that have plagued the United States, among them carp, pigeons, starlings, English sparrows, kudzu, brown marmorated stink bug, emerald ash borer, European gypsy moth, woolly adelgid, the Burmese python, European brown rat, and many hundreds of others, with more arriving every year.

Wineberries make for great pies, cobblers, and jams.

Indeed, the phrase *invasive species* has strong, negative connotations among folks today… and rightfully so. Yet, on the other hand, other invasive species have become some of the most welcomed arrivals in America, so much so that people have even forgotten that these flora and fauna are strangers to our shores. Consider the earthworm and the beloved honeybee. Among the others that boast positive images are the ring-necked pheasant and brown trout. And what would today's barnyard look like without such aliens as chickens, cows, horses, and house cats? Just where does the wineberry fit in?

Why the Wineberry Arrived Here

Rubus phoenicolasius came here as an ornamental plant, and some garden companies still sell it today. A close relative of the blackberry and raspberry, which share the genus *Rubus*, the wineberry quickly became naturalized and began to spread. As an ornamental and a plant, the wineberry sports many attractive features.

One of these traits is the reddish thorns, which are shorter and much less sharp than those of raspberries and especially of blackberries, which flaunt a painful barb. The thorns of wineberries are more like bristles, so picking berries is not such a prickly affair. As is true with raspberries and blackberries, the berries grow on canes, which can be over six feet long. So long, in fact, that they often bend down and touch the ground.

The leaves are the standard green on top, but the undersides are a silvery white which typically become very visible before a thunderstorm or any time when the wind blows. The blossoms are white but so small and discreet that they are easily missed—a real contrast with the more showy white blossoms of blackberries.

Developing berries are anything but discreet as they undergo a color metamorphosis. The first stage is when a brown case encloses the berry, which when it emerges is green, then, in turn, becomes yellow, orange, and red when ripe. I keep close watch on our many wineberry patches after the berries have turned orange, because they are a popular menu item for such game animals as deer, bears, and turkeys as well as raccoons, opossums, and skunks, plus many species of songbirds. In our backyard, I have observed whitetails and squirrels feeding on wineberries; on our 38-acre parcel, I once came across a hen turkey and her poults that were feasting on these fruits. Nevertheless, despite my fears of being outcompeted for these delicious red berries, there always seem to be enough for the wildlife and Elaine and me.

The red berries deserve further description. They are noticeably smaller than a blackberry and a tad bigger than a raspberry. The little "cups," known as calyxes, which the berries reside in are very similar to those of a raspberry and the fruits can be removed fairly easily. Berries have a "sweet stickiness" to them, so I find that I am constantly wiping my hands on my pants. I would describe the fruit's particular shade of red as more of a scarlet hue.

The taste, oh that taste, is divine. Wineberries are sweeter than raspberries and dramatically more so compared to the tart blackberry. The secret pact I make with myself on every wineberry picking excursion is that the only berry I will consume is the last one I pick on the outing. Otherwise I would never make it home with enough berries for Elaine to create the pies, cobblers, and jams that she concocts from them.

How to Regard the Wineberry

No doubt exists that the wineberry provides important food and cover for wildlife and that humans find it delicious as well. But, scientifically, how should we regard this *Rubus* family member? Lindsay Thomas, director of communications for the Quality Deer Management Association (QDMA), a leading conservation organization, offers this perspective.

"There are two kinds of non-native plants," he said. "The first kind offers no value and no one wants them around or plants them. The second kind is a species that through misunderstandings or for whatever reason has had certain 'experts' encouraging people to plant it. A good example of the second kind is the autumn olive. It offers food and cover, but often at the expense of native plants.

"At QDMA, our position is to not encourage the plantings of non-natives, like the autumn olive, even if they have benefits. We feel that native plants should be given first consideration when landowners are thinking about planting something. For example, many native plants exist that will do a far better job of providing food and cover than autumn olives, and they won't get out of hand on a property like autumn olives so often do. We have seen places where autumn olives created such a thick over story that nothing grows beneath them"

Thomas says that the benefits of wineberries are very similar to its close relatives such as the blackberry and raspberry and those two are the plants that a landowner should favor. I then asked Thomas if we should try to eradicate the wineberry or curtail its growth in an area.

"That depends on a lot of factors," he said. "Are the wineberries crowding out raspberry and blackberry vines? Is there a lack of food and cover in an area and wineberries are providing that? How does the individual landowner feel about the presence of wineberries? The dynamics are often different everywhere and what decision is made comes down to the individual landowner's perspective."

Elaine gathering wild wineberries near our house. Note the long sleeve shirt and pants to help protect against insect bites.

If landowners do not want to use chemical-based methods, the removal of invasive plants is often very difficult to accomplish, says Thomas. One way that some invasive plants can be held back some is by frequent mowing. Another way is by controlled burns during the growing season. For more information on how to manage your property, Thomas recommends the "Plant This, Not That" section of the QDMA website: www.qdma.com/articles/plant-this-not-that-habitat-improvement. On a personal note, I am a member of the QDMA and find the habitat improvement articles extremely beneficial regarding decisions I make on our land.

Like the vast majority of non-native species, the wineberry is here to stay. Whether readers decide to embrace, eliminate, or tolerate it is a personal decision.

15. Grapes

The species of grape that grows in our woods, the summer grape, is one of the most common in America, thriving in the entire east and also west to Texas and Kansas and even growing in California. But the summer is just one of many wild grapes that flourish across the country (more than 50 species exist), and one or more varieties grow just about everywhere in the United States.

Summer grapes ripen in late summer or early fall in much of their range.

Grapes feature perennial climbing vines, and although they are not a colonizing plant (that is a plant like blackberries that moves into an area after soil disturbance such as fires and logging), they often spring up in an area some five to ten years after a change has occurred. Songbirds poop out the seeds, which helps to spread grape species. Once grape vines become established, they can live for a very long time. I've observed them growing deep in the forest, but also thriving at the edge of woods, as well as on trees, shrubs, and fencerows.

The stems have a "shredded" look, the tendrils are always looking for something to latch onto, the green leaves are heart-shaped and lobed, and the fruits are, of course, purple. The summer grape should probably be called the early fall grape, as they ripen in my area around mid-September.

Good grapevine patches are uncommon, and I watch over mine, beginning in early September as all manners of birds and mammals are attracted to them as well. As soon as the berries turn purple, Elaine and I will journey to the prized patch, a stepladder in hand. Some of the lushest growth is at the top of the vines. I don't like to be more than about 10 feet off the ground, but the vines can wind up a tree as tall as it grows. Last, if the grape crop has been abundant, berries may still be edible for humans well into November. Many times while hunting, I've stopped at a grape arbor for a quick, Vitamin C-rich snack. By December, though, grapes are little more than dried raisins.

16. Wild Black Walnuts

Sometime in September, across much of the range of the wild black walnut, its nutmeat will begin to ripen. If for some reason, you don't remember that date, just follow where the local squirrels will be heading as their destinations will likely be the nearest walnut groves.

Wild black walnuts add zest to bread and cookie
recipes and go great in oatmeal, too.

Juglans nigra grows over the eastern half of the country from Vermont to northern Florida, west to eastern South Dakota, and down to central Texas. Wild walnut trees thrive in the limestone soil that makes up my Southwest Virginia property, several especially doing well at the site of an old homestead. But this species also grows well on sandy or silt soils, and truly flourishes in stream bottomlands and along fencerows where it can become the dominant species.

Increasing the Yield of Wild Black Walnut Trees

One of the easiest ways to increase the yield of wild black walnut trees is to conduct TSI (Timber Stand Improvement). Last winter, for example, I cut down competing trees around one of our wild black walnuts. This enabled the tree to spread its crown and produce more nuts for autumn.

Joel Pedersen, the National Wild Turkey Federation's director of western initiatives, touts TSI.

"In doing TSI, you are eliminating trees that you don't want competing with trees that you do want," he said. "Cutting these less desirable species can result in the favored tree having less competition for nutrients and sunlight and thus producing more mast and better quality timber in the case of the black walnut.

"Black walnuts are very slow growing and long lived [often surpassing 100 years], like many oaks, so TSI can very much benefit their growth. Another thing that landowners can do is fertilize along the drip lines of these trees."

Be careful when conducting TSI that you don't mistake walnut trees for the invasive paradise tree, also known as tree of heaven or ailanthus, which has similar long, pinnate, compound leaves. For example, once while removing trees from around a favorite wild black walnut, I mistook a young walnut for an ailanthus. The worst part of cutting down the sapling was that it was growing far enough away from its likely parent tree that both could have thrived.

Two ways to tell the two species apart are the presence of the paradise tree's samaras (winged seeds) in the spring and its cantaloupe-like bark in color and appearance. The bark of a walnut tree is a darker gray and furrowed.

Nutritional Benefits of Black Walnuts

When Elaine was recovering from breast cancer, walnuts were one of the foods that clinical nurse specialist Laura Pole, who operates Eating for a Lifetime, encouraged her to consume. A major reason why, says Pole, is because of the nutmeat's essential fatty acids, particularly Omega 3s and 6s.

This nut is also a good source of protein, minerals, dietary fats, Vitamins B6 and E, antioxidants such as manganese, and heart-healthy unsaturated fats. See www.eatingforalifetime.com.

Gathering, Cracking, and Storing Walnuts

When ripe, walnuts sport a light greenish yellow to brown outer husk, which should be removed as soon as gathered. A few times, I stored the nuts with the husks on and doing so negatively affected the taste of the nutmeat. When gathering and removing the husks, I recommend wearing gloves and old clothes as the husks can stain anything they come into contact with. A few whacks with a hammer can effectively remove this outer barrier. Also, do not leave the husks anywhere near a garden or plants, as a chemical in all parts of this tree can have a toxic effect.

After husk removal, I store the nuts in a cool, dry place for a fortnight, in this case our basement where a dehumidifier runs. From Elaine's and my experience, this curing process seems to bring out the rich, nutty flavor. When cracking, we use three things: a cinderblock, hammer, and pick. Several light taps with a hammer is usually sufficient to loosen the nut wall, and a pick simplifies the nutmeat extraction. We refrigerate the nutmeats and try to use them within several months. If this sounds like a great deal of work, well, it is.

However, the intense, high flavor of wild black walnuts is worth the effort as the nutmeats add real zip to breads and cookies. We enjoy the taste of walnuts that we purchase from the grocery store, but we relish the flavor burst that we receive from the wild version.

Walnut Trivia

- At various times, walnuts have been used to ward off witches and those with the "evil eye."
- Walnut wood is highly valued for furniture. A professional logger offered us quite a bit of money if he could harvest our mature walnut trees. We turned him down.
- Walnut trees are toxic to tomatoes, potatoes, and many berries and other plants and trees as well. That's why we don't cultivate domestic trees in our yard/garden area.
- Some Native American tribes used walnut bark and husks to poison fish for harvest.

Thousand Cankers Disease

Originating in the West, Thousand Cankers Disease has been identified as a major threat to black walnut trees; other species of *Juglans* are affected as well.

"A number of tree species can get canker diseases," says Pedersen. "Canker diseases are often specific to certain species, stunting their growth and sometimes killing them."

The walnut twig beetle (*Pityophthorus juglandis*) causes these cankers (which are areas of diseased tissue) and result in later attacks by a fungus as well. Early symptoms include yellowing and wilting of upper branches which relentlessly spreads to lower ones. Death can occur in just three years. The affliction is spreading eastward. For more information: www.walnutcouncil.org.

17. Pawpaws

Pawpaws are a fascinating shrub or small tree that grows across most of the eastern half of the country. They thrive in damp creek hollows, river and creek bottoms, or cool hollows on the side of a mountain or hill. I often see them growing as understory trees on our land and other places as well. Pawpaw leaves are long, fairly narrow, and smooth sided; some folks call them elephant ears because they can extend outward as much as a foot. The bark is quite dark and usually smooth.

Pawpaws don't remain on the ground for long as
wild animals relish these fruits, too.

Where the pawpaw becomes rather quirky in nature is in regard to its fruit, which can be quite large—eight ounces or more. Pawpaw fruits are green for most of the time they are on trees, but when they start to ripen in mid-to late September where I live, they develop yellowish sections and even black blotches here and there. If they fall to the ground, you can forget about gathering any because just about every wild mammal relishes the sweet fruits.

Perhaps sweet is not quite the right word — *sickly sweet* best describes the smell and taste of a pawpaw which can overwhelm my sense of smell and taste. Eating one ripe pawpaw out in the woods is a delightful experience; consuming two — not so much. For the same reason, cooked pawpaws should be eaten in moderation; we almost always turn them into bread or cookies.

If some of the pawpaws are not quite ripe when you gather them, watch over them closely. Because when they do ripen, they do so quickly and will just as quickly rot. Some folks call pawpaws "mountain bananas," others give them the appellation of "poor man's custard." Whatever they are called, pawpaws are among the most fascinating trees in the forest.

18. Persimmons

Elaine picking wild persimmons on a late autumn afternoon. We don't like to share the locations of our favorite persimmon trees — the fruit is that delicious.

I would be hard pressed to state whether summer grapes or persimmons are my favorite fall fruits, but if forced to choose, the nod would have to go to the persimmon. The orange golf ball-size globes feature a pleasant but not overpowering sweetness when they ripen in late October and early November. Eat one in September, though, and your mouth will pucker in a most unpleasant way as if you swallowed a ball of cotton.

Persimmon trees feature a dark bark that is laid out in little square blocks, which make identifying the trees quite easy. The leaves are about 4 inches long, shaped like an elongated egg, and quite smooth on the sides. The trees thrive in much of the lower two-thirds of the East; I most often find them along fencerows and overgrown fields.

Interestingly, one winter when I was cutting downed trees for firewood, I came across a lone persimmon tree surrounded by non-mast bearers. Rambling across more of our 38 acres, I found two more persimmon trees. I then cut down the surrounding, non-mast bearers so that the persimmons could receive more sunlight, expand their crowns, and produce more fruit.

Finally, here's a trick that Elaine and I learned when preparing persimmons to bake as part of bread or cookies. Place the fruits in a large strainer and press down on them with a tin can. This forces the pulp out through the strainer and saves much preparation time.

Persimmon bread and cookies cooling on the Ingram's kitchen counter. We love how dark persimmon bread looks and how great it tastes.

19. Hickory Nuts

On our land, three species of hickory trees grow: shagbark, mockernut, and pignut. The pignut nutmeat (which is the proper term) tastes fine, but the flavor of the shagbark and mockernut far surpass it. Many folks may not know that the most popular member of the hickory family is the pecan, which generally is considered to have the best flavor and is the star of pecan pie. The only problem about gathering and cracking shagbark and mockernut nuts is that you will rarely have enough nutmeat to make them the main part of any recipe requiring nuts. So Elaine and I will just add a few spoonfuls of hickory nuts to any recipe requiring nuts.

Pignut hickories have tasty nut meats, but its close relatives, the shagbark and mockernut, feature even better nuts.

Several other species of hickories exist, and as a group one or more species grow in states in the eastern half of the country. As a group, the trees have compound leaflets that are long and pointed. For example, the shagbark and pignut usually has five to seven leaflets, the mockernut seven to nine. The shagbark is best distinguished by, logically enough, its shaggy bark growing in semi-detached strips on the tree. Older mockernut trees have bark with deep furrows. Interestingly, the leaves of this species are very aromatic when crushed, which is a really good diagnostic feature.

The nut-husks, generally, are a yellowish-green and fairly hard to crack, but the meat, such as it is, is quite good. Only you will be able to determine if the great effort is worth it.

20. Fruit and Nut Recipes

Wild Berry Pie Recipe

(works equally well with blackberries, dewberries, raspberries, or wineberries)

Ingredients

1	prepared pie crust, both top and bottom crusts
1	qt. of wild blackberries, dewberries, raspberries, or wineberries
⅔	cup sugar
½	tsp almond extract
2–3	Tbsp King Arthur pie filling enhancer for thickening
3–4	drops of King Arthur Fiori di Sicilia
1½	Tbsp butter

Directions

Preheat oven to 425°F.

Place pie crust in the pie pan. In a bowl, combine berries, sugar, almond extract, pie filling enhancer, and Fiori di Sicilia. Stir to combine and pour the mixture into the pie crust. Chop the butter into pea-sized pieces and dot them over the fruit.

Top the berry mixture with the top pie crust. Cut several vents in the top crust to allow steam to escape. Bake at 425°F for 15 minutes.

Then reduce the heat to 375°F and bake further for 38 to 40 minutes until the top crust is golden brown and the fruit is bubbling. The pie will set up better if allowed to cool at least ½ hour before serving.

Notes

We have also used tapioca as a pie thickener, but the pie filling enhancer does a nice job with watery fruit.

Wild Berry Cobbler

Ingredients

1	quart fresh wild berries
⅔	cups sugar
½	tsp almond extract
3	scoops of King Arthur pie filling enhancer
3–4	drops King Arthur Fiori Di Sicilia
1	stick butter or margarine
1	cup flour
¼	tsp salt
2	tsp baking powder
1	cup milk

Directions

Combine the berries, sugar, almond extract, pie filling enhancer, and Fiori Di Sicilia and set aside. Elaine's pies and cobblers were great before, but when she started adding the pie filling enhancer and Fiori di Sicilia, they went to another level. Then in a small bowl combine the flour, salt, and baking powder. Stir in the milk with a wire whisk until well blended. Set aside for 2–3 minutes. Melt the butter and pour into the bottom of a 2-qt. baking dish. Pour the batter over the melted butter. Next pour the fruit mixture over top of the batter, spreading the fruit out to the edges.

Bake at 375°F for 40 minutes. Check the center for doneness—if doughy, cook a little longer.

Note: For blackberry pies and cobblers, we use 1 cup sugar. But the inherent sweetness of wineberries and raspberries enables us to use just ⅔ cup.

Wild Berry Jam

This recipe should make 7 cups of jam, so plan accordingly when gathering jars, lids, and screw bands. You will need a boiling water-bath canner and familiarity with home canning. Home canning directions are included in boxes of fruit pectin.

Ingredients

	Enough wild berries to make 5 cups when crushed
4	cups sugar
1	box fruit pectin

Directions

Put the crushed fruit into a 6–8 quart pot. Combine ¼ cup of the sugar with the box of fruit pectin. Stir this into the fruit in the saucepot. Bring this mixture to a full rolling boil, stirring constantly. Stir in the remaining sugar quickly. Return to a full rolling boil and boil exactly 1 minute. Keep stirring. Remove from the heat and skim off foam, if any. Ladle into the prepared jars, adding lids and screw bands, and process in a boiling water bath according to your canner's directions.

Wild Berry Pancakes

Ingredients

½	cup milk
2	Tbsp melted butter
1	large egg
1	cup flour
2	tsp baking powder
2	tsp or more sugar
½	cup blackberries or other wild berries

Directions

Mix together all dry ingredients in a bowl. Combine the egg, butter, and milk. Add to the dry ingredients, mixing well. Fold in berries. Cook on a hot griddle until both sides are done.

Wild Berry Waffles

1½	cups all-purpose flour
½	cup whole wheat flour
3	Tbsp sugar

1	Tbsp baking powder
½	tsp salt
1¾	cups milk
1	Tbsp oil
2	large eggs
½	cup wild berries

Directions

Combine all ingredients in a large mixing bowl. Allow mixture to rest about 5 minutes while waffle iron preheats. Use ½ cup batter at a time and cook until golden according to the directions on your waffle iron.

Wild Grape Jelly

Ingredients

4	cups grape juice
7	cups sugar
½	bottle liquid pectin

Directions

To make the juice:

Remove the grapes from the stems. Sort and wash them well. Crush the grapes, place them in a saucepan and add enough water to cover. Bring to a boil on high heat. Reduce the heat and simmer for about ten minutes.

Strain the mixture through a strainer to extract the juice. Place the juice in a refrigerator to chill. The next day when you're ready to use the juice, strain a second time through cheesecloth to remove any tartrate crystals that may have formed.

If you didn't find enough grapes to make a quart of juice, measure the juice that has been prepared and adjust the sugar and pectin proportions accordingly.

Follow the directions for the pectin product you have, but generally this is what to do:

Measure the juice and place in a large pot or kettle. Stir in the sugar. Cook over high heat, stirring constantly, until mixture comes to a full rolling boil—meaning one that can't be stirred down. Add the pectin, bring to a boil again, and boil for 1 minute.

Remove from the heat and skim off any foam that is on top. Pour into sterilized jars and follow the directions for sealing the jars by the water-bath method.

Elaine and our daughter Sarah hard at work on an early fall day: from left to right, venison roast simmering in a slow cooker, Sarah putting the finishing touches on jars of summer grape jelly, and canned venison jars cooling.

Elaine's Whole Wheat/Wild Black Walnut Banana Bread

Makes 1 loaf

Note: This same recipe can make great persimmon or pawpaw bread, just substitute the persimmons or pawpaws for the bananas.

Ingredients

½	cup butter
⅔	cup brown sugar
1	egg
¾	cup unsifted whole wheat flour
¾	cup unsifted white flour
1	tsp baking soda
¾	tsp salt

1¾	cups mashed ripe bananas
¼	cup buttermilk or yogurt
½	cup wild black walnuts, roughly chopped

Directions

Preheat oven to 350°F

Grease a standard loaf pan

Cream butter until light. Add sugar and cream until light and creamy. Beat in egg.

Sift together both flours with the soda and salt, and set aside. In a separate bowl combine the mashed banana with the buttermilk or yogurt.

Add the dry mixture to the creamed butter alternately with the banana mix. Stir just enough to mix well. Fold in walnuts.

Pour into the greased loaf pan.

Bake for 50 to 60 minutes or until done. Cool in the pan 10 minutes, then remove and allow loaf to completely cool on a rack.

Persimmon Cookies

Ingredients

½	cup butter
1	cup sugar
1	egg
1	tsp. vanilla
2	cups flour
½	tsp baking soda
½	tsp baking powder
¼	tsp salt
¼	tsp each of cloves and nutmeg
¾	tsp cinnamon
¾	cup dried cranberries
1	cup black walnuts
1	cup persimmon pulp

Directions

Preheat the oven to 375°F.

Allow the butter and egg to reach room temperature. In a separate smaller bowl combine the flour, baking powder, baking soda, cloves, nutmeg, and cinnamon. Stir to combine.

When the butter is softened, cream it in a mixer. When light and fluffy, add the sugar and mix. Next add the egg, then the vanilla, beating well after each addition. Gently mix in the persimmon pulp.

Add the dry ingredients to the batter, mixing thoroughly. Then fold in the cranberries and nuts. Besides wild black walnuts, we've also used shagbark and mockernut hickory nuts from the trees that grow on our land. These hickory nuts go great in either persimmon cookies or bread.

Drop by the rounded teaspoonful onto a cookie sheet lined with parchment paper. Flatten the cookies slightly with your fingers.

Bake at 375°F for 12–13 minutes. The recipe makes about 4 dozen cookies.

Elaine with a fresh batch of persimmon cookies.

Pawpaw Cookies

Several tidbits about using pawpaw pulp in recipes. Pawpaws taste great in the field and in bread and cookies. But I have found, as have other family members, that for whatever reason, they are best eaten in small doses. So no matter how good that first pawpaw in the field is, don't eat another. And no matter how tasty these first two cookies are, don't try a third.

Ingredients

1½	cup pawpaw pulp
¾	cup softened butter
1⅓	cup sugar
1	egg
3	cup sifted flour
1	Tbsp baking soda
1	tsp salt
¼	tsp ginger
¼	tsp cloves
1	tsp nutmeg
1	tsp cinnamon
⅔	cup walnuts

Cream the shortening and sugar thoroughly. Add beaten egg and pawpaw. Stir in the dry ingredients, which have been sifted together, and mix well. Form into small balls and place on cookie sheet. Press into round flat shape. Bake in a 350°F degree oven for 11–12 minutes.

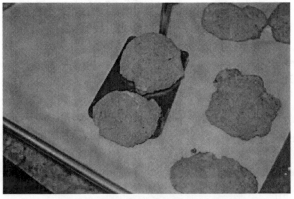

Pawpaw cookies hot from the oven.

21. Mushrooms

A number of wild, edible mushrooms exist, and two of the more popular are morels and oysters. Morels (of which numerous varieties exist, such as the white, black, and tan) typically only are found in the spring, especially during rainy periods. Morels feature a spongy top, hollow stems and caps, and a height of one to five inches. I typically find them when I am spring gobbler hunting or fishing for native trout in mountain streams.

In Southwest Virginia and Southern West Virginia, where I am mostly afield come spring, morels often seem to grow in tulip poplar groves, moist field edges, and old orchards. Tote your morels home from the woods in mesh bags so that the thousands of spores that exist in each cap can escape as you walk—perhaps allowing other morels to pop up eventually.

Noted Virginia outdoorsman Jim Crumley rates oyster mushrooms as one of his favorite species and says that one of the best things about the variety is that the oyster can be gathered year round.

Oyster mushrooms can be gathered throughout most of the year.

"Oysters often grow on hardwood stumps that have started to decay," he says. "I also find them on standing, dead poplar trees, usually high up instead of close to the ground like many mushroom species. And mature red cedar trees growing in a pasture could have oysters under them, as can small hollows or along a creek. But, then, sometimes none of these type places will have oysters growing; they really are a mushroom that you sort of find them where you find them."

Crumley strongly urges that novice mushroom hunters go afield with a veteran gatherer as well as a printed field guide. He recommends the *National Audubon Society Field Guide to North American Mushrooms* and Michael Kuo's *100 Edible Mushrooms*. North America has many varieties of benign as well as poisonous mushrooms, and some species, such as the infamous Destroying Angel, can be deadly. Longtime mushroom seekers often say that nothing looks exactly like a morel or oyster, but a novice may not be able to note those traits that distinguish an edible variety from a poisonous one—hence the advisability of starting out with an experienced instructor who is familiar with the fungi found in your area.

Oyster mushrooms feature a broad, appropriately enough, oyster-like appearance that could be eight or nine inches or more across. This "wavy" species can be white, gray, tan, or brown. Oysters are a variety that freezes well, unlike morels which do not from my experience.

"Drain the oysters in a colander until dry," says Jim. "Then scissor them into small bits over a frying pan on medium heat with butter and chicken broth. Cook for a few minutes, let cool thoroughly, and put them in a freezer bag."

Recipes

Jim Crumley says one of his favorite ways to dine on oysters is as part of scrambled eggs. Here is Elaine's and my favorite morel dish.

Wild Turkey Leg Salad with Morels

Ingredients

	Turkey legs
3	stalks chopped celery
½	cup chopped mild onion

3	chopped hardboiled eggs
½	cup mayonnaise
	Salt and pepper to taste

Directions

In a pressure cooker, place two wild turkey legs and add water. Raise the pressure and cook for at least 45 minutes and allow pressure to drop on its own. When ready, the meat can be pulled from the bone.

Separate meat from bones using your fingers. Be careful to not let any slivers of leg bones slip by.

To the meat, add 3 stalks chopped celery, ½ cup chopped mild onion, 3 chopped hard boiled eggs, and ½ cup mayonnaise. Stir well, adding salt and pepper to taste. (We prefer sea salt and freshly ground black pepper.) You can add optional, supplementary ingredients of your choosing: cranberries, grape halves, and chopped nuts (especially wild black walnuts or shagbark hickory nuts).

Wash and chop mushrooms then sauté them in butter until tender. Be careful not to overcook as morels will become mushy. Drain on paper towel and let cool, then stir into salad.

This salad is great on top of mixed greens or even as a sandwich.

Finding morel mushrooms is a highlight of
any spring trek through the woods.

IV. How to Grow a Backyard Garden

Growing a backyard garden can be as simple as someone with a patio apartment growing a few tomato plants in containers, or as involved as someone turning their entire backyard into a vegetable paradise. The first step to undertake is to have your soil tested. This is done by scooping up dirt from various places in the yard and then sending the samples to your local extension office.

The three main nutrients that an extension office analyzes are nitrogen (N), phosphorous (P), and potassium (K). After the results are analyzed, the office will recommend fertilizers that can amend the soil for the vegetables that you want most to grow. Generally, you will want the Ph of your soil to be between 6.0 and 7.0, which is fairly neutral (the scale runs 0–14). This sounds simple, and it is, but the harder part is nourishing the soil.

I also want to suggest doing something before you continue with your labor—build a fence around your garden, and string wire around the entire perimeter. This wire should be hooked to some sort of device (Elaine and I use a small solar powered box that resides on a platform attached to a fence post). Otherwise, you could perform a great deal of work and just when you're about to harvest your crops, some creature (deer, raccoons, skunks, opossums, or many other creatures) could undo your work in one evening. I know that's possible, because it has happened to me.

For nourishing the soil, we have turned this task almost entirely over to our chickens. As soon as the last vegetables are harvested for the year, usually in October, we start dumping the chicken manure and straw from our two henhouses into the garden. Then several times weekly, we turn the chickens into the garden (our two chicken runs are located next to—and share one common fence with—the garden).

Our birds delight in churning through the soil; through their non-stop scratching, they naturally work in their own manure and straw (meanwhile emitting more poop as they work) into the soil. In the process, they dig up and ingest all manner of noxious insects, insect egg cases, and weeds. The chickens enjoy this so much that they will even whine to me to "go next door" if they see me open the gate to the garden. Frankly, we've had the best gardens of our lives since we started raising chickens.

Understandably, if you don't have chickens, you'll have to do this labor yourselves. Be sure to work in lots of organic matter (leaves, grass clippings, and composted food –our compost bin is located near our garden). I prefer to use organic fertilizer which is typically made from animal and plant matter (manure and compost) as opposed to industrial chemical fertilizer. Since chicken manure is so high in nitrogen, I select organic fertilizers that have higher phosphorous and potassium ratings than nitrogen ones.

Quality gardens often begin with a soil test.

What to plant depends on your personal preferences, and, unfortunately, what your garden site will grow. We chose as our house site the one part of our property that lies in a frost pocket, which wasn't very smart but we just didn't know any better. The good news is that we rarely have to use an air conditioner in the summer, the bad news is that the soil warms slower come spring. For whatever reason, our soil doesn't grow good potato crops, but strawberries thrive.

So readers likewise will have to determine what plants, and varieties of them, will grow best. County extension agents can help somewhat, but experimentation will be needed. And here's one final tip on starting. Mulch your garden (straw is a good choice), which means, spread some sort of organic material around the base of the plants. This will help keep weeds out (saving you hours of hoeing) at the same time it keeps moisture in (saving much water).

Besides strawberries, we grow onions, tomatoes, squash, zucchini, asparagus, and sometimes spinach and the odd green pepper plant. Our garden is not very large, roughly 25 feet by 25 feet, but it supplies us with some of our summertime vegetables, and that's good enough for us.

22. Fruit Tree Option

In our backyard, we have two North Star cherry trees, one Dolgo crabapple, and three apple trees: Grimes Golden, Black Twig, and Rome, with the Rome being the only apple tree producing fruit, as the Grimes and Black Twig are quite young. Only one of the North Star trees is old enough to produce cherries; we enjoy this variety so much that we planted a second tree as a backup source in case something happens to the first one. Bear populations are high in our area, and though we have metal cages around our trees, that won't necessarily stop a bear from entering a cage and devastating a tree. They can strip a tree of fruit, while breaking its limbs with their sheer bulk.

Dolgo crabapples may taste rather tart straight off a tree,
but in breads and cookies, they are scrumptious.

At this writing, the Dolgo crabapple is only five years old but it produces a goodly amount of very tart fruits that are superb in breads, cookies, and, to our surprise and joy, jellies. The three apple varieties are all heritage ones, which means that they came into existence well before World War II. In the years before the war, and even more so afterwards, many apple catalogue companies decided to emphasize fruit appearance instead of taste. The variety that most exemplifies this sorry turn of events is the inaptly named Red Delicious, which, though it has a pretty color and handsome shape, tastes like moist cardboard. We enjoy heritage apple varieties and order new trees from those mom and pop orchardists that still carry the traditional ones. You can certainly order the modern varieties; many are quite good, most are rather mediocre, and too many are gosh awful.

One of our heroes in the heritage apple cause is Virginia's Tom Burford, who wrote *Apples of North America: 192 Exceptional Varieties for Gardeners, Growers, and Cooks*. One of Tom's disciples is Charlotte Shelton, whose family operates Albemarle Cider Works and sells heritage varieties as well. She shared this inspirational story on how she and her family became devotees of traditional apples.

"Both the Burford and Shelton families are from Albemarle County, Virginia so I had known Tom all my life," says Charlotte. "One weekend in the early 1990s, Tom was leading an apple tasting at Monticello, and I had the chance to taste some of the varieties and talk with him. I was so inspired that I bought two trees each of ten heritage varieties that he recommended. The next year we bought 25 varieties and 50 trees.

"By 2000, the family's hobby had evolved into a business—thanks to Tom's help and inspiration, which have been unstinting. We now make and sell cider, put on workshops, and graft and sell heritage trees. A very important aspect of the business for us is helping to promote and preserve heritage varieties that don't have traction in the commercial world but that are very worth promoting—and that have merit for biodiversity as well."

For the benefit of those readers who may want to start or add to their heritage orchards, I asked Tom and Charlotte to detail some varieties that would thrive in various regions and climates and would fulfill various niches in the usage department. Keep in mind that Burford's book goes into much more detail than is possible here.

- Albemarle or Newtown Pippin...Thrives in the Blue Ridge region but also in California, the Pacific Northwest, Hudson Valley, and Midwest. Superb for dessert, baking, pie making, vinegar, and cider.

- Criterion…A great choice for much of the West Coast, originated in Washington. Used as a dessert apple, drying, and in salads.
- Chehalis…Originated in Washington, often a favorite variety for organic growers because of its disease resistance. Super as a dessert, baking, and pie apple.
- Carter's Blue…An early tree thrived near Montgomery, Alabama, does well in areas of deep South, a fine dessert apple.
- Roxbury Russet…Perhaps the oldest named variety in America. Originated in Massachusetts and thrives throughout much of the Northeast. Great for drying, pies, and cider.
- Baldwin…A favorite throughout New England as an all-purpose apple, especially good for pie making, cider, and desserts.
- Ben Davis…At one time, extremely popular in the Midwest. Known for its excellent storage qualities and for cider and drying.
- Grimes Golden…Originated in West Virginia, grown throughout the Mid-South, an excellent pollinator and a fine all-purpose apple. One of Elaine's and my favorites for pies and applesauce. A small apple that has a hint of cinnamon-like flavor.
- Stayman…Originated in Kansas, will also do well in any mountain climate. Known as a superior dessert apple and for pie making, apple butter, frying, applesauce, and cider. Elaine's favorite apple and in my top three, behind only the Black Twig and Grimes Golden.

Here are some of the words of wisdom that Tom Burford communicated to me and that can help beginning and veteran backyard growers.

- ✓ "Of course, I want my book to inform people, but mostly I want to inspire the readers. If someone comes to me and wants to learn how to prune correctly, I can tell them. But that individual won't really learn how to prune until he actually experiences it."
- ✓ "I've often experimented with various techniques involving apple growing because I was curious. Some of my experiments have proved disastrous but I've learned from them."
- ✓ "I'm in my 80s and some of my experiments will take another 20 years to play out. I'm looking forward to being around for the outcome."
- ✓ "A key question every American should be asking is how will we feed everyone when the world population doubles in 50 years? There will be more people to feed and less land available. Our current industrial

food production method is unsustainable. Look what is happening right now in California with the water crisis."

✓ "Too many Americans believe that we have to go to the supermarket to obtain our food. No, we do not."

✓ "More and more parents are coming up to me and saying that they want to know what's inside the food they bought at the supermarket before it is fed to their children. That is a very good sign."

✓ "If I know the manager of a supermarket and he is present, I will go there and write TOM on the top of those heavily waxed Red Delicious apples. He'll say, 'Tom, you know, I can't sell that now.' "I'll say, 'that was my point.'"

✓ "Respect the regional nature of apples. Many varieties won't reach their full potential when they are grown outside of their home areas."

✓ "Don't ever buy store apples on sale."

Look Critically at an Individual Tree... Several years ago, several of my young apple trees had been devastated by an attack from 17-year-locusts. As is the habit of this species, the females had cut slits in my fruit trees and laid eggs there, horribly weakening the limbs. I pruned the trees but they were still sickly. Tom's advice?

"Two tips," he said. "If you are expecting an outbreak of 17-year-locusts or any kind of disease, don't plant trees that year. People worry about losing a whole year of tree growth, but that's a small thing compared to the damage that locusts or some diseases can cause.

"Second, prune a young tree that has been heavily damaged back to about a foot above the graft. I know that that sounds severe, but getting rid of all that dead wood and disease damage will allow the tree to respond with lots of young, healthy growth."

Burford told me that he was once touring an orchard as part of a seminar he was giving. When the group arrived at a young tree that had been heavily damaged by some affliction, someone asked Tom what should be done to help the tree. Tom took out his pruners and reduced the tree to the size of a whip.

"The crowd gasped when I did that, but later the orchard's owner told me I had done exactly the right thing," said Burford.

More tips:

✓ *Plant trees that traditionally have done well in your region...*When I first started growing heritage apple trees, I wanted to try a number of the most famous varieties, one of which was a Magnum Bonum.

But this variety is best suited for elevations below 1,500 feet, and I planted it on some mountaintop land of mine that lies at about 2,500 feet. Predictably, the tree did poorly, never producing an apple and eventually dying. In his book, Tom recommends trees that will grow well in various regions. No matter how appealing the description of a variety might be, he says, don't plant a tree that is not suited for living in a particular region. Doing so is a waste of time and money.

✓ *Know your local diseases*…Yet another mistake I made when I began planting trees was not knowing the most pernicious diseases in my area, perhaps the worst of which is cedar apple rust, common in the Smoky Mountains. I planted several varieties that were highly susceptible to this plague and the results were predictable.

✓ Tom said this is a common mistake that backyard growers make and one that can be avoided by our doing a little research. Tom's advice comes from experience. He once spent several years trying to prune a tree that had been racked by fire blight. In the future before I purchase a variety, I will read the section on "disease resistance" that is included with his descriptions of each apple in *Apples of North America*.

✓ *Prevent deer damage*… During Elaine's and my visit with Tom, we were hosted by Charlotte Shelton and her family, which operates Vintage Virginia Apples and Albemarle Cider Works in North Garden, Virginia. Of course, we had to tour the Shelton's orchard where I noted small concoctions hanging from strings on all the trees. Tom and Charlotte explained that what I was seeing was Milorganite. Milorganite is a bio-solids fertilizer that comes from the Milwaukee Metropolitan Sewerage District. Both apple experts proclaimed that it was the best thing that they had found to ward off whitetails. Charlotte also added that squirrels can be a major problem for orchardists, and the solution she has found to keep these rodents away is a dog. One of her pooches is so antagonistic toward bushytails that he catches and consumes them.

✓ "What destroyed America's original apple culture were the large mail order companies taking control of the orchards. Those companies controlled what was planted, which fractured the entire regional and local apple culture. I want to recreate that culture. Global warming will change which varieties we grow in certain regions."

23. Apple, Crabapple, and Cherry Recipes

Crabapple Nut Bread

Ingredients

½	cup butter
⅔	cup sugar
2	eggs
2	Tbsp milk
½	tsp lemon juice
2	cups flour
½	tsp sea salt
1	tsp baking soda
2	cups roughly chopped crabapples (leave the skins on, but remove the core and seeds)
½	cup chopped nuts

Directions

Cream the butter and sugar.

Add eggs, milk, and lemon juice.

Mix flour, salt, and baking soda together; add to butter mixture.

Stir in the crabapple and walnuts until combined.

Grease a large loaf pan.

Add batter and bake at 350°F for 55–60 minutes or until a toothpick inserted in the middle comes out cleanly.

Cool then slice.

Crabapple Jelly

Crabapples have natural pectin, so when using the juice from the apples it is not usually necessary to add commercial pectin.

Ingredients

3	lbs crabapples
3	cups water, approximately
4	cups sugar

Directions

First prepare the crabapple juice. Cut the blossom ends and stems from the crabapples, then cut the apples into small pieces. Put in a saucepan and barely cover with water. Bring to a boil, then reduce heat and simmer the apples until they are soft, about 20–25 minutes. Place a sieve over a large bowl or pot and line the sieve with cheesecloth. Pour the fruit mixture into the sieve and allow the juice to strain through.

Measure the juice into a kettle, then add sugar. If the juice amount is 4 cups of juice, 4 cups of sugar is the correct amount. For less juice adjust sugar accordingly.

Cook, stirring regularly, until the mixture sheets from a spoon. Pour into clean hot jars and process in a water bath according to the canning directions for both your altitude and the size jars used.

Grimes Golden Applesauce

The quantity of apples does not really matter, but when we make applesauce we usually make enough to last for several days at a time. Just about any variety of apple can be turned into applesauce, but Grimes Golden, a famous heritage variety that originated in West Virginia, is our favorite for this purpose.

Ingredients

1	peck Grimes Golden apples
¼	cup sugar or more depending on taste
¼	cup water

Directions

Peel and slice the apples. Place them in a heavy pot, allowing room for the apples to steam and bubble as they cook. Add ¼ cup or more of sugar. We prefer the natural sweetness of the apples so we feel little sugar is necessary. Add ¼ cup water and stir.

Cook the apples over medium heat until the apples start to sizzle. Then reduce heat to medium low, cover, and let the mixture continue to bubble. The apples will begin to get tender. Occasionally mash them with a potato masher. Apples will continue to cook and soften, approximately ½ hour. We like our applesauce chunky so at this time we stop cooking and store the mixture in the refrigerator until eating, but you can mash the sauce more finely if desired. You can also try additions such as cinnamon or vanilla.

Note from Bruce: Elaine likes just a little cinnamon and no vanilla with her applesauce, while I like lots of both and a sprinkle of nutmeg. Experiment to see what you prefer.

Rome Apple Nut Bread

Rome apples are a heritage variety known for being a superior baking apple. The apples from our backyard tree make a marvelous nut bread, and, of course, many other varieties do as well.

Ingredients

2⅓	cups all-purpose flour
⅔	cup whole wheat flour
1	tsp baking soda
1	tsp salt
1	tsp cinnamon
¼	tsp baking powder
3	eggs, beaten
1½	cups white sugar
½	cup packed brown sugar
⅔	cup oil
1	tsp vanilla
⅓	cup of wild black walnuts or hickory nuts
3	cups peeled, shredded apples (about 4)

Grease two 8 × 4 × 2-inch bread pans or three 7½ × 3½ × 2-inch pans.
Heat oven to 325°F.

Combine all dry ingredients except sugars in a medium bowl.

In a large bowl combine oil, eggs, sugar, and grated apple and mix. Then add flour just until moist.

Bake for 45 to 55 minutes at 325°F. Test with a toothpick.

Homemade bread made with Rome apples from the Ingram's backyard.

Elaine's Cherry Pie

We have two North Star cherry trees growing in our backyard, and they make scrumptious pies and cobblers. These tart cherries typically ripen in mid-to-late May in our area of Southwest Virginia and are disease-free. Conventional wisdom says to use tart cherries only in pies and cobblers. In this case, conventional wisdom is correct.

Ingredients

4	cups tart cherries (4 cups after pitting)
¾	cup sugar
1	tsp almond extract
½	cup King Arthur's Pie Filling Enhancer for thickening
2	prepared pie crusts, either from a favorite crust recipe or commercial pie crusts
2	Tbsp butter

Directions

Line a pie pan with one crust. Combine the cherries, sugar, pie filling enhancer, and almond extract. Stir and pour into the pie crust.

Dot the fruit mixture with the butter chopped into pea sized bits. Then put the second pie crust on top, sealing the edges well. Cut several slits in the top of the crust to allow steam to escape.

Bake at 425°F for 10 minutes, then at 375°F for approximately 40 minutes more, until crust is golden brown and the fruit is bubbling. If you can wait long enough to eat it, allowing the pie to cool makes for prettier slicing.

Note: I put my pies on a thin round metal plate to bake to prevent spillovers from getting in the oven, and I use a pie ring that I place on top of the crust while baking so the outer edges of the pie don't get overly brown.

V. Getting Started on Chickens

Elaine and I started raising chickens in the spring of 2011. One of the reasons for wanting to do so is because Elaine is a breast cancer survivor, and she hired Laura Pole, a clinical nurse specialist who operates the service Eating for a Lifetime, to help her develop a better diet so that the odds would be less that cancer would return. One of the foods that Pole told her to avoid was meat from animals that had been factory farmed because of the estrogen-based growth hormones. And the nutritionist, besides encouraging Elaine to buy free range or organic chickens for their meat (which we have been doing), also told us that those same chickens produce eggs high in Omega-3 fatty acids, which offer health benefits for cancer survivors—as well as, obviously, the general public. So we made the plunge to begin our chicken raising careers.

Like any new venture involving animals, much preparation had to occur before our two-day old chicks were to arrive. My biggest fear was that given my inexperience with tools, I wouldn't be much help with designing and building the coop. Elaine, though much more adept with building things than I am, worried that she wouldn't be able to design a run that would keep out predators.

It was then that we decided that if we worked cooperatively based on our strengths, perhaps they would overcome our shortcomings. Our first step was to visit the local Southern States Cooperative where we met the resident poultry expert, Lynn Sowers. She showed us copies of the books *Storey's Guide to Raising Chickens* and *Chicken Coops: 45 Building Ideas for Housing Your Flock* (by Judy Pangman).

These two excellent books greatly broadened our knowledge of chickens and gave us ideas on how to design a coop that would be just right for our backyard.

A locavore lunch anchored with eggs from our chickens, zucchini and onions from our garden, and persimmon nut bread.

Next, it was time to start the run, and here is where we were able to use one of my strengths—knowledge of the outdoors. I am an avid hunter and frequently pursue deer, turkeys, squirrels, and other game behind our house. I have observed no fewer than 13 different predators there, ranging from raptors (hawks and owls) to omnivores (raccoons, opossums, skunks, coyotes, foxes, bears and bobcats) to the creature I feared the most in terms of attacking our chickens (minks). See next chapter for detailed information on predator-proofing chickens.

Elaine knew that I would be little help in figuring out or implementing the chicken house plans, so she enlisted friend Ken Rago, who is a "tool guy." Elaine and Ken studied plans from Storey's *Chicken Coops* and together they came up with a concept that looks something like a doghouse. The front of the coop features a door that can swing down for a gang plank; the back a window for aeration that can be opened to access the three nesting boxes. Running from side to side within the house are two wooden perching rods.

Elaine estimates that she and Ken spent 14 to 16 hours planning and constructing the coop. My major contribution came after the house was finished. I noticed that they had positioned chicken wire over the window, and I feared that a black rat snake could slither through the wire one night. I located an old window screen, cut a rectangle out of it, and stapled that over the chicken wire. Later, I added hardware cloth on the window and door, as it is much stronger and offers more protection.

Selecting a Breed

I grow heritage apple trees and understand the importance of keeping alive those old varieties. So it was only natural that I would want to rear heritage chickens as well. I recalled that my Grandmother Maude reared Rhode Island Reds (RIR), so that was what we selected.

The RIR originated in Rhode Island and Massachusetts in the 1880s and 1890s and has long been known for its hardiness and its ability to be a dual purpose bird (great at producing eggs and meat). Jennifer Kendal of the American Livestock Breeds Conservancy (ALBC), which works to conserve rare breeds and genetic diversity in livestock, says that first-time chicken raisers might want to consider such heritage breeds as Buckeyes, Dominiques, New Hampshires, Javas, and Delawares. For more information, Kendall suggests this link: www.albc-usa.org/heritagechicken/chickencomparison.html.

"Heritage breeds in general are good choices for anyone who rears poultry," she says. "Heritage or traditional chicken breeds often retain essential attributes for survival and self-sufficiency such as fertility, foraging ability, longevity, maternal instincts, ability to mate naturally, and resistance to disease and parasites. These were the chickens raised by our grandparents, and their grandparents, on small farms throughout the country."

It was only after I had communicated with Kendall that I realized that we had not ordered heritage RIR. See Chapter 25, "The Heritage Chicken Option."

"Typically, people end up with the production Reds," she told me. "It's getting harder and harder to find the old-type Rhode Island Reds, and they are typically obtained through breeders. [Readers] can join our organization, but they can also view our website which has an online directory of our members that they can search.

"They can then contact these individuals to arrange for purchasing eggs or chicks or in some cases adult birds. If readers want to purchase from a hatchery, they should be prepared to ask questions of the hatchery such as—do your birds meet American Poultry Association standards? What selection practices do you employ?"

May 4—The Chicks Arrive

"We've got chicken nuggets," beamed Elaine as she lofted a cardboard box (that looked like a Happy Meals container) through the car window.

I was working on lesson plans during my planning period at the school where I teach when the office called and said that my wife wanted to meet me in the parking lot.

"I've got to hurry home and put the chicks in their new home," she announced and at that drove off down the highway. A few hours later, I joined Elaine to observe ten 2-day-old chicks inside a Rubbermaid container, a heat lamp affixed to the side, pine shavings on the bottom, and a chick feeder and waterer within. Young chicks have to have a setup like this, as their feathers are too undeveloped to keep them warm.

Lynn Sowers had told us that if we wanted gentle future hens and roosters that we handle the chicks often, but also to make sure that we always wash our hands in hot, soapy water before and after to prevent transmitting or receiving germs. So after scrubbing, we did as Lynn had instructed, which the chicks did not seem to mind. Indeed, even now, we try to touch every chicken every day, which is one reason we think the birds are so calm and friendly.

Everything went well for the first few days as the chicks both ate and slept a great deal. We even checked them during the night and became used to seeing them active at all hours. But on the morning of May 9, one chick seemed sluggish and later that day it died. The next day, another chick acted lethargically and Elaine called Sowers who told us that the chicks might be suffering from coccidiosis (an intestinal disease that chicks often contract) and gave us some medicine to put in the waterer. I also administered it to the sick chick through a medicine dropper. I awoke at 2:00 A.M. to give the chick some more medicine only to find it dead. What had we done wrong?

"Nothing at all," consoled Sowers. "It's normal to lose two or three out of every ten chicks. Sometimes the cause is coccidiosis, sometimes something else, sometimes they were just the runts of the litter."

Reassured, we continued to talk to and touch the chicks often and marked each week of their lives with pictures. When they were three weeks old, I began feeding them stink bugs that I had caught outdoors, and we were constantly entertained about how excited they were to catch and then try to eat a stinkbug—which was quite a mouthful—before another chick stole it.

It was about this time that we identified our first rooster, Little Jerry, which had received his name from the luckless cock in a *Seinfeld* episode. Little Jerry was always the first to explore something new that we placed inside the Rubbermaid container and also to approach a stinkbug that had been dropped inside.

June 15—Moving to the Coop

Sowers had also told us that the chicks would have developed enough feathers to live outside when they were five to six weeks old. So when our young charges, which we now called "teenage chicks," were five weeks old, we began bringing them to the run for a few hours at a time. On their initial visit, they were terrified of their new surroundings and spent much of the time sitting on Elaine's lap. Only Little Jerry would venture very far away from her and then only a few feet.

But by June 15, the six-week marker had arrived, and we placed our no-longer-small juveniles in their new home. The entire first day went smoothly but when night came, none of our young chickens knew what to do in terms of entering their coop. Finally, as darkness descended, Elaine and I decided that we would have to pick each one up and place them inside the coop. After that night, the process leading to roost time was fairly predictable. Several of our chickens would linger on the gangplank leading to the coop, then finally walk inside. Others would hesitate outside, enter, then exit the coop, repeat the process and finally go in to stay. Little Jerry would enter the coop last, walk out, make a quick ramble around the perimeter of the run to make sure everyone was safely inside, then enter for the night.

Successes and Failures

At six months of age, our pullets (hens less than a year old) began laying eggs—cause of great celebration. Let me share our successes and failures.

Success: *Attending a workshop for novice chicken raisers.* We learned a great deal about chick and chicken care and what materials we would need.

Failure: *Buying straight run chicks.* Even though we could have purchased ten hen chicks, we wanted the experience of raising hens and roosters and also of having a rooster in the barnyard to protect the hens. But we ended up with six roosters and two hens. We traded one rooster for several dozen farm fresh eggs, ate four more, and kept Little Jerry. With only two hens in our original flock, we had to purchase three 16-week-old RIR hens.

Success: *Solar power electric wiring around perimeter of run.* Three times during those early months, I heard a wild animal squall in the vicinity of the run, likely from having contacted the electric wires.

Failure: *We were not happy with the strength of chicken wire in terms of thwarting a determined predator.* But every other wire we looked at featured openings that a mink or opossum could slip through. Finally, we decided that our next chicken run would have both chicken wire (because of the ultra-small holes) and stronger wire fencing inside that. We have been pleased with that setup on the second coop we built.

Success: *Elaine and I closely working together on a project.* Raising chickens is a marvelous way for couples to spend time together.

24. Protecting Your Flock

When Elaine and I decided to raise chickens, we talked to the two other families on our Botetourt County, Virginia rural road who had done so. Both had free-ranged their chickens and both had had their entire flocks wiped out. One family had this happen several times. Though free-ranging sounds great, Elaine and I thought it was impractical given the rural nature of our area and our 38 wooded acres with a creek.

This is great wildlife habitat, but also great predator habitat. So we decided to predator-proof our chicken run as much as possible. In short, in our area and in many others as well, at least thirteen types of wild animals are threats to chickens. It's extremely important for chicken owners to understand how, when, and where these marauders will attempt to attack. Here are some ways to predator-proof your run against these animals.

Winged Raiders

Two categories of winged raiders exist, those that pillage by night and those that do their work by day. On our land, we have two of the most typical nighttime predators in the form of screech and great-horned owls. (Note: some areas will no doubt also have barred and barn owls.) A chicken rearing acquaintance told me about the disturbing experience she had when early one morning, she alarmed a screech owl that was standing over a mound of feathers, all that remained of a hen. Earlier one evening at dusk, she had spotted a great-horned owl perched on a tree in her yard, and her flock soon featured one less hen.

Among the daytime predators we have are the red-tailed and broad-winged hawks, which are in the buteo family. That means they feature broad wings and stocky builds and are best suited for swooping down on rodents (think mice, rats, and squirrels) in small openings. But a buteo is also an opportunistic feeder and will certainly attack a chicken if the situation arises.

The other major category of hawk is the accipiter clan. We occasionally have an accipiter visit our place, primarily Cooper's hawks, but the chance sharp-shin passes by, too. Traits that characterize an accipiter are slender bodies, short rounded wings (which result in incredible mid-air maneuverability), and long tails, which also contribute to maneuverability. Sharp-shins are fairly small and are not major chicken predators, but the same cannot be said about the larger Cooper's.

I once observed a sharp-shin nabbing a goldfinch from our bird feeder—a prime reason why we stopped feeding birds, as we were really only operating a menu line for the hawks. Given their respective body constructions, accipiters are far better than buteos at snatching birds out of mid-air; but since chickens rarely fly, this trait is largely irrelevant to backyard poultry enthusiasts.

What is relevant is how to protect against both the day and night winged invaders. Lynn Sowers, who is the resident poultry expert at the Botetourt County Southern States Cooperative, told us that the easiest way to thwart avian attacks is to string netting (the same kind used to prevent songbirds from eating fruit from an orchard) over a chicken run. Sowers added that over the years she has been constantly amazed at how few people were willing to do this or even thought to do so.

Elaine and I found it easy to position netting over our run. All we had to do was to nail some 2 x 4s atop our run's posts, position the netting, and then "anchor" it by using twist ties. Periodically, we check to see if small openings in the netting have occurred. One such breach occurred when a heavy, wet snowfall (which caused the netting to bow) resulted in some of the ties loosening. It was a simple matter to replace them.

Mammalian Threats

Of course, the major threats to backyard chickens are mammalian thieves. All of them are more likely to attack at night than during the day, but some, such as the coyote and fox, could show up in the daytime as well. In addition to coyotes and foxes, the other members of this rogue's gallery are bears, minks, skunks, opossums, raccoons, and bobcats. Here are the steps we took to thwart them.

- After we sunk our foundation posts in concrete, we strung galvanized chicken wire fencing with small, hexagonal openings (1-inch). We attached it with ¾-inch galvanized fencing staples. Later we put stronger wire inside this as sort of a double barrier. We also later positioned 19 gauge galvanized hardware cloth with ½-inch openings, which is both more durable and stronger, on the doors of our two runs.

- By far, the best precaution we took to protect our chickens was to position two strands of solar powered electric wires around the perimeter of our run. The first strand is about six inches off the ground, the second a foot. When winter snow storms and summer thunderstorms have left us without power for up to two days, our solar panel has kept humming and kept our birds safe. Many, many times at night, I have been awakened by the sounds of raccoons bawling in our backyard, no doubt from having come into contact with the hot wires. Once the electric fence repelled a black bear. Even other large mammals, such as coyotes and bobcats, would receive considerable shocks when touching the wires. I know that I receive a distinctly unpleasant charge when I accidentally lay a hand on a wire.
- Out from the perimeter, Elaine and I positioned on the ground yard-wide strips of hardware cloth, anchored with 2 x 4s and rebar. Over the top of the wiring, we placed bricks and cinderblocks for more weight and deterrence. One thought that comforts us is that even if a predator tunnels under the prone wire, it would almost certainly come into contact with the lowest strand of electric fencing when the animal ventured close to the main fence.

Our next step was to build a sound henhouse with a lock on the door and a double screen window. Another chicken-rearing friend of ours has lost a number of chickens over the years. He says he likes to let his birds "put themselves to bed" at night—meaning the door to his fenced run is open so that the birds can free range, as is the door to the henhouse. Our acquaintance even told us that one morning he found a very full opossum sleeping in a nesting box. In Elaine's and my opinion, this lack of security is inexcusable. Our run door is always kept locked at night. As soon as our birds enter their house for the night, we latch them in. The house's back window has layers of screen and hardware cloth that have been stapled to the inside and outside. The structure itself rests on cinder blocks to prevent rotting of the wood and something eventually boring through.

Of course, there are other steps you can take to protect your chickens. One acquaintance of ours has taught his dog to believe that the chickens are the canine's personal possessions. The pooch loyally watches over the chickens during the day and his doghouse is just a few yards away at night.

The first year or so we raised chickens, our rooster Little Jerry was a very efficient guardian of our flock. Little Jerry crowed when any creature, human or animal, came into our yard. Once he bit off the head of a snake. Another time he emitted an alarm call that sent the chickens running for cover (a hawk had flown over). He would have, without a doubt, given his life to protect his harem.

However, Jerry also became extremely aggressive toward Elaine and me, repeatedly attacking her and once severely pecking me. We tried all kinds of behavior modification (bending his head downward on his chest so that he would learn to be submissive to us) but nothing we tried proved permanent. In the end, Jerry had to be dispatched.

Protecting your chicken flock begins with sturdy housing
and fencing, plus netting and electrified wires.

More Strategies

Besides dogs and roosters, we recommend several other actions that can decrease the chances of predation. For example, several years ago (before we began raising chickens) a bear repeatedly visited our compost bin at night. I had the idea to put the bin inside our fenced-in garden, which Elaine claimed was an incredibly bad notion — that the bruin was so enamored with the goodies in the compost bin that he would surely do anything to reach them.

My spouse showed foresight as the very first night the compost bin was inside the garden, the bear broke down the fence to reach the container and even left a steaming mound of scat as his calling card. My point is that nothing which can attract a predator should be left inside or near a run. That means that you should also bring in your chicken feeder at night and, for example, not position something like a bee hive near your run.

Another step we took was inviting a professional trapper to come to our land every winter and decrease the predator population. One winter the gentleman's best haul included a fox. We also have one of those have-a-heart style boxes positioned near our run. Occasionally we catch raccoons and opossums that have decided to check out the perimeter. These pillagers are dispatched the following morning.

Recently we had a poultry rearing friend catch an opossum in her trap and then she drove the creature, still inside the trap, "well out in the country," she said and released it. In many states, this type of action is illegal and only gives your problem predator to someone else. Be sure to check with your local conservation officer before setting any kind of trap. Find out what you legally can and cannot do.

I want to emphasize that Elaine and I are not against free-ranging chickens. In fact, we often put our flock in the garden from mid-fall to mid-winter. We also will release them into the yard. But these walkabouts are always supervised by us. We enjoy interacting with the chickens at this time, tossing them bread crumbs, and letting them entertain us. But we never leave them alone outside.

Elaine and our son Mark also made a chicken tractor (a portable, covered chicken run; ours is about a yard wide and five yards long), which we keep in our front yard. Some afternoons, our birds will spend a number of hours inside, busily "mowing" that section of yard for us. Still, we occasionally look out the front window to see if our birds are safe, and we keep a window open so that we can hear a distress call. One day, for example, we saw a black vulture perched on the tractor, suspiciously eying our birds.

I also want to stress that our setup, and any setup known to man, is not foolproof. My greatest concern is that the two predators I fear the most—a black bear and a mink—will one day risk the electric fencing and burrow under or cut through the perimeter, or in the case of a bear especially, just bull its way through the defenses. But in the meantime, Elaine and I are going to try to keep our chickens as safe as possible and continue to explore ways to make our defenses strong.

25. The Heritage Chicken Option

Most chicken breeds sold at feed stores or shipped by mail to homes are not really Barred Plymouth Rocks, Delawares, Buckeyes, or whatever name they go by, but hybridized versions of the original, heirloom breeds. So I began a search to find a breeder of heritage Rhode Island Reds, which led me to Brice Yocum, who operates Sunbird Farms outside Visalia in California.

"We love to help people interested in heritage chickens," he said. "Our farm was established to help preserve heritage American breeds. We have heirloom RIR and Buckeyes available from some of the finest and oldest lines in America."

The reference to *lines* needs to be explained. Birds that are heritage must be "from parent and grandparent stock of breeds recognized by the American Poultry Association (APA) prior to the mid-20th century; whose genetic line can be traced back multiple generations; and with traits that meet the *APA Standard of Perfection* guidelines for the breed." Lines are heritage chickens that individual breeders have raised.

Yocum further explains the concepts of a line.

"A line is a closed breeding program typically associated with heritage livestock," he said. "It is often named after the person or persons that have devoted a number of years to developing and breeding for specific traits. There are approximately five lines of RIRs worth having in America, and mine is one of those lines. Not all heritage chickens come from closed lines, for example, our Buckeyes.

"They are from Chris McCary, president of the American Buckeye Poultry Club. Chris has been working with these birds for a number of years, and has derived stock from the American Livestock Breeds Conservancy (ALBC), a source for preserving heritage livestock in America.

"When looking for any heritage poultry, I look for birds that have been cared for by breeders who have a commitment to a particular breed. I want conformance to what I call Standards of Performance, meaning *performance* in the areas for which these dual-purpose birds were originally created. You have to remember, these birds weren't created for the show ring, though they can thrive there, but they were created for the farm."

In May of 2013, Elaine and I ordered five, 8-week-old heritage Rhode Island Reds from Yocum.

"My chickens come from a line known as St. Augustine that is now in the hands of Ron Fogle," said Yocum. "Fogle got his original birds from Jacob Bates, who got them from his father Ricky. This line has not been crossed with any other line for 15 to 20 years."

Obviously, line breeding involves breeding hens and roosters that are related. Is there a danger of genetic deformities occurring?

"My experience with line breeding has been that genetic problems don't usually occur," said Yocum. "I think you can have enough genetic diversity if you don't breed chickens that are related too closely. In working with heritage lines, you can get worse genetic problems if you combine birds from different lines.

"I also like to breed birds from the same line where the birds have lived in different parts of the country and have evolved certain traits that make them successful in that particular region's climate. For example, I live in California and you live in Virginia. In five years, I might want you to ship some of your Reds to me for breeding with mine."

Our grandson Sam is fascinating by our heritage
English Buff Orpington chickens.

Advantages of Heirloom Breeds

Yocum stresses that heritage birds possess many positive qualities that industrial birds lack.

"Production Reds have been raised just for egg production," he said. "After two years, they can experience a sharp decline in egg production. Additionally, this intense breeding for egg production can result in birds with poor temperaments and lacking in meat quality."

Conversely, heritage Reds, and other heirloom breeds as well, can be consistent egg producers for many years. And the roosters can have much more friendly dispositions around people, confirmed Yocum. He also acknowledged what Elaine and I had learned the hard way—that industrial Reds, as well as many other production breeds, typically have no concept of how to sit on a nest and brood young, whereas heirloom birds often make fine brooders and mothers.

"Right after World War II, chicken breeders started selecting for either egg production or meat production," said Yocum. "And there were some disastrous consequences. For example, the Cornish chicken was originally a great meat bird that did well on pasture. Now the Cornish cross birds often will eat themselves to death if you don't take their food away. They also grow so big so fast that their bodies can't support their weights.

"The Cornish cross lives virtually in a contained structure, raised with significant amounts of antibiotics as if it were in a hazmat situation. The birds are so lacking in natural immunities that any disease that is introduced can wipe out an entire population. Now, the Cornish cross produces the vast majority of chicken meat in this country, but at what cost."

Yocum adds that if a widespread disease epidemic hit the industrial chicken business, heirloom breeds might not be as susceptible to the plague.

"Heritage birds are used to feeding on bugs and green foods," he said. "The young chickens I shipped you have been on pasture since shortly after they were born. They have built up a natural immunity to many things that would otherwise be dangerous to industrial flocks. In short, heritage birds help provide a stable food and egg source in the event of a disease outbreak."

Yocum says that each of the heritage breeds bring something different to the proverbial table.

"Buckeyes are top-shelf meat birds that thrive in both cold and warm climates. Rhode Island Reds are a classic dual-purpose bird that can live in a variety of climates, produce good numbers of eggs, and taste great. Both adapt easily to wherever they live and are natural foragers.

"Delawares are also wonderful heritage birds. They have a solid, meaty frame and plenty of egg laying prowess. They are great foragers, willing to work for their food, and keep the farm free of pests."

Yocum waxed almost poetic about what he calls the "quality of the product."

"Heritage chickens *taste* like chicken, and heritage eggs *taste* like sunshine and grass," he said. "The biggest reason for raising these breeds, the reason preservation is so important, beyond diversity and food security, is that America has lost the complex and enriched flavor profile of heritage foods. Heritage chickens, in contact with the earth, with greens, with sun, with bugs, are the best tasting, most healthful kind of chicken you can eat.

"You can see it in the rich orange color of the yolks and taste it in every bite. Pastured poultry is lower in fat and higher in Omega-3s."

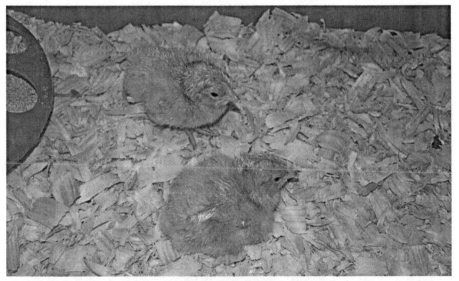

Once you get started on chickens, you will find them a utilitarian creature.

Of course, most production birds raised on pasture and/or in our backyards can excel as meat birds or as egg producers just like their heirloom counterparts do. My industrial Rhode Island Reds did yeoman service in the two-plus-years Elaine and I owned them. They provided us with healthy eggs, tasty meat, garden manure, yard pest control, and hours of entertainment. We simply came to want something more from the experience of raising chickens: hens that could brood their own eggs and raise their own young, plus our helping out in the preservation of America's heritage breeds.

The Beauty of Traditional Chicken Breeds

Traditional breeds not only perform marvelously well as meat, egg, or dual purpose chickens, they also often sport a vibrant appearance.

"Heritage Rhode Island Reds have almost a brick shape," said Yocum. "They have a fairly flat back, a nice vertical keel, and a flat bottom. Their color is darker than brick, not exactly black, though, more of a rich mahogany."

The intense coloration of our heritage birds was apparent as soon as Elaine and I removed them from their shipping box. Two of our industrial birds have a light brown appearance, and two others feature a mostly brown one. The intense mahogany hue of our heritage quintet is stunningly beautiful.

Summing Up

I want to emphasize again that despite the flaws of our industrial Reds, Elaine and I have genuinely and profoundly enjoyed raising them. Each bird has exhibited an individual personality, added something to the flock as a whole, and the hens have produced excellent numbers of eggs—though, as noted earlier, production noticeably declined not long after their second birthdays.

Heritage fowl are for those folks who want to experience the next level of raising chickens, who want to become acquainted with the type of birds that our forebears raised, and who want to keep alive for future generations the unique qualities that make traditional breeds an integral part of Americana. Perhaps you might want to become one of those people who raise heritage chicken breeds. For more information, see:

American Buckeye Poultry Club: www.americanbuckeyepoultryclub.com

American Livestock Breeds Conservancy (ALBC), www.albc-usa.org

American Poultry Association: www.amerpoultryassn.com

Brice Yocum and Sunbird Farms: www.sunbirdfarms.com

Farmers' markets are sublime places to practice a locavore lifestyle.

V. The Joy of Hunting and Fishing

A Letter to My Grandson Sam

Dear Sam,

I don't know how old you will be when you read this, but I want to tell you about the events of the summer of 2015 when you turned three years old and I was 63. That was the summer that your dad and I decided to introduce you to the pastime of angling. But there was so much more to our plans than merely fishing, as wonderful a pursuit as it is.

We had much discussion on how to proceed. For three straight mornings, your dad and I decided to show you the many joys associated with angling. The first morning, we went down to the creek behind the houses where your family and your grandmother (you called her *e-mama* that summer because you had trouble pronouncing *g*s) and I live. You were in charge of carrying a blue minnow bucket and a small yellow "dipping" bucket that previously had served you well in your sandbox. Your dad toted a seine, and our mission was to corral the various aquatic creatures dwelling in the creek and show you the indescribably joyful pleasures of a stream brimming with life.

Your dad held the seine, and you and I (holding your hand) charged through a shallow riffle, kicking over rocks and sloshing through the water toward the net and having a grand time doing so. I saw your wide-eyed wonder when we examined the net and observed minnows, sculpins, crayfish, and even a young smallmouth bass within. I began the years-long process of explaining the roles of each of these organisms in the ecosystem — that smallmouth bass were predators and that one day we would fish for them; that minnows and sculpins were crucial to the cycle of life and thus just as important as bass; and that crayfish held incorrectly would pinch. I knew that day that you would not remember those initial lessons, but one future day you would start to comprehend. After about 25 minutes, your dad and I sensed that your attention span was waning (you spotted some child's long lost dump truck on the bank and wanted to play with it), and we then had you release the teeming bucket of creatures back into the creek.

Our son-in-law David and grandson Sam seining
for minnows in the creek behind our house — what a
joyful and wholesome way to spend a summer day.

The next morning the three of us went to my garden and dug through the soil looking for live bait. I wanted you to feel a sense of ownership in this endeavor and you certainly did. Again, you had your yellow sand bucket in tow, and I let you use a trowel to sift through the dirt. It was a dry summer day, and we were only able to dredge up a few earthworms and grubs (you were fascinated with the former and slightly frightened by the latter), but it was enough bait for the next day. Again, we only spent about 25 minutes on an activity, not wanting boredom to set in.

The next day we drove to a small lake that possessed everything a small child would need for a first fishing expedition: a bountiful bluegill population, and docks to sit on. You watched as I tied on a hook and affixed a bobber to the line. You were assigned the crucial job of holding a pair of red clippers, used to snip the tag end of the line from the hook's knot.

Finally, it was time for you to begin your actual fishing career. Your mom, e-mama, and one-year-old brother Eli watched from the shore as you, your dad, and I walked out to a prime spot on the dock. Sam, you had a little trouble not wanting to swish the line and bobber back and forth, but soon your dad instructed you on the value of patience and waiting and preparing for good things to happen—a life lesson for sure. Soon enough you settled down and began intently staring at the bobber. An overly aggressive four-inch bluegill found a sliver of worm appealing, the bobber began dancing, and before long you and your dad derricked the sunfish up onto the dock.

"I caught a fish," you screamed and your dad beamed and I laughed long and hard. Hesitantly, you picked up the bobber with one hand and tentatively touched the fish with the index finger of the other hand. Then you announced that you wanted to catch another one. After your dad released the bluegill and cast the line, you sat down between his legs and with great intensity locked your eyes on the bobber. Again, it began skipping about, dipped under the water, and you, sort of, helped your dad set the hook.

This time, you wanted to show off your catch to Eli, and from his stroller, he tried to clasp the wriggling bluegill in his hands. Your sense of pride and accomplishment were a wonder to behold. After you caught one more fish, you announced that you wanted to go to the nearby swing set, and your first fishing trip was over after about 25 minutes. Your dad and I were proud of you, and I confess to being grateful for such creatures as small, hungry bluegills.

Sam, over the years to come, I want to teach and show you, and soon enough Eli, so much about the wild world and life. I want to show you how to still hunt for squirrels, cast a spinning rod for river smallmouths, and a fly rod for stream trout. I want to sit with you high in a tree stand and watch as you draw a bow on your first whitetail. And sit beside you, while you, trembling, watch a turkey gobbler striding in, gobbling at every step, eyes alert for the slightest movement.

Sam and his granddaddy Bruce baiting
up for a morning of fishing.

More importantly, I want you to become a conservationist, to know the inherent values of woods, soil, air, waters, and wildlife. That these life-affirming things are worth defending and protecting. I want us to stand side by side to plant trees, pick wild berries, and gather nuts, and also to roam the woods, wade creeks, and float rivers. To study wild creatures, learn bird songs, and identify trees and plants. To become a part of the wild world and be content, joyous, and thankful while there.

But most of all, Sam, I want you to be a good and caring person, to fall in love with someone some day and become a good husband and father. I want you to find satisfaction in a worthwhile job and treat your co-workers with respect. I hope to be along for a good portion of your life's journey and be there when you need me.

Love,
Granddaddy

The Fascination Began at Five

At the age of five, I began a lifelong fascination with the magic of moving water, sneaking away from my parents' house and slinking down to Gish's Branch (an incredible distance of 150 yards) where I seined minnows with a window screen. Minnows with brightly colored sides, I labeled rainbow trout; every minnow with fat sides, I called a sunfish; every other finned beastie was lumped into the generic category of bass. I also built small rock dams where I corralled creatures and was always mystified when they had not stayed put after I came back a day or two later.

By the time I was nine I had begun riding my red Schwinn a whole mile down to a Roanoke River tributary, which Gish's Branch emptied into. For a few glorious weeks, I caught chubs and redbreast sunfish by dangling chunks of worms (several rainy mornings they had made the mistake of lingering too long after sunrise on our driveway) beneath a golf-ball size red-and-white bobber. But I soon became desirous of bigger quarry.

A peer had regaled me with tales of incredibly sized fish—he called them smallmouth bass—that reached a fantastical 10 inches and finned in a pool another half-mile distant from home. I became obsessed with taking this trek and finally succumbed to the wanderlust that exists in many young boys—and no doubt in many girls as well.

I arrived at the pool one sunny Saturday morning and hurled a gob of crawlers toward the heart of the hole. I reasoned that bigger fish would want bigger bait, not a bad maxim really. However, a sycamore intercepted the squirming mass—something that trees inexplicably still do today. Unfortunately, this sycamore was no ordinary one as a hornet's nest resided in its lower limbs, and the winged attackers soon found the source that had disrupted their universe.

Covered in stings, I knew that I would not be able to conceal from my mother's prying eyes what had happened. Since my parent's wrath was now assured, I decided to move downstream, catch some sunfish, bring them home, and demand that I wanted them for dinner.

My parents did not like fishing or fishermen. Earlier, Dad had pronounced, "Boy, you'll never make any money fishing," and mom had said that all fishing would earn me was "bee stings and snake bites," and she was half right already. Both had proclaimed that fishing was the pastime of idlers, wastrels, and ne'er-do-wells.

Of course upon my arriving home, Dad whipped me with several prime switches cut from our forsythia (it was debatable whether the stings or the switching hurt worse) but Mom cooked the sunnies. Depression-era survivors, they felt it was a sin to waste good food.

Afterwards, and after much reflection and nursing of my many wounds, I came to one of those proverbial forks in the road…whether to obey my parents' commands regarding fishing or blatantly disobey them. The words from Mark Twain's *Huckleberry Finn*, spoken by a boy about the age of me, neatly sum up my dilemma and what fork I decided to take.

> *I was a-trembling, because I'd got to decide, forever, betwixt two things, and I knowed it. I studied a minute, sort of holding my breath, and then says to myself: "All right, then, I'll go to hell."*
>
> *It was awful thoughts and awful words, but they was said. And I let them stay said; and never thought no more about reforming.*

So as soon as a respectable amount of time had passed after the hornet incident, I resumed sneaking away to ride the Schwinn down to the creek. The problem became, though, that I could not catch any of the smallmouths, causing both my frustration and my fascination and obsession with this game fish to grow.

Day after day I would hurl the conglomeration of worms out to the finning creatures and day after day they would ignore the mass. I have always suspected that my parents knew I was disobeying their strictures, but they seemed to have come to a tacit understanding that I could not be dissuaded from going fishing. It was as if they had given up hope of my ever having a respectable hobby.

Five years passed and I became adept at catching rock bass, redbreast sunfish, and even chain pickerel, but still no smallmouths. It was then that I sought out the wisdom of a very worldly 16-year-old, practically a man, who had been rumored around school to have caught a half-dozen or maybe even more bronzebacks during his long, angling career. His name was Rick and he also possessed a car, a blue 1957 Ford station wagon, that gave him access to a countryside far more remote than what I could travel to on my Schwinn.

Rick promised to take me stream smallmouth fishing, and on a May Saturday we deposited our rods (mine the classic Zebco 33 spincasting outfit, his one that I had never seen but had heard about—a spinning rod) in the station wagon. Rick's destination was the same creek which was my home water, but his favorite fishing hole was ten miles farther away and up and over a mountain—a trek I could never have accomplished on my bike.

When we arrived, Rick proudly opened an Old Pal tackle box and inside was an incredible array of fishing gear. The box contained the same types of bobbers, hooks, swivels, and sinkers I possessed, but also flaunted what seemed an astronomical number of lures, six in fact, that Rick explained his dad had given him over a period of years. They included three Mepps spinners with gold, silver, and bronze blades (my mentor instructed that he used different colored blade baits for different colored water), two Daredevil red-and-white spoons, and something he called a Shyster spinner that sported squirrel hair attached to its treble hooks.

Rick offered to let me use the Shyster but warned that I would have to pay him two bits (a quarter) if I lost it. He then tutored that I was to fan cast—a new term to me that Rick explained meant casting to a different spot each time in a systematic manner—the spinner.

For some 45 minutes, we hurled our respective lures around the creek with my Shyster producing no better than Rick's Daredevil. But the whole experience was intoxicating to me as surely this was the euphoria that came with being part of the adult world of fishing.

And then the life changing event occurred. I felt a solid thump on the line, the Zebco rod bowed, and yards away a monstrously sized fish cleared the surface. Rick yelled "Big smallmouth on," and I frantically horsed in the leaping, lunging creature, beached it, and grabbed the flopping fish.

The 16-year-old took a tape measure from his tacklebox and soon pronounced that the smallie measured 9 inches, a lunker for sure. Rick also declared that I was to release the smallmouth, as the species was not to be casually creeled like sunfish and chubs, that bass were special and could be caught over and over again, perhaps even by me. Trembling, I freed the brown bass, an experience that made me feel good inside and hopeful that I would indeed catch that same fish again. The release also had the tangential benefit of eliminating the evidence that I had been fishing.

I immediately offered to buy the Shyster from Rick; he declined saying that I couldn't possibly have enough money to acquire the lure, but after wrangling for some minutes, I finally purchased it for 50 cents. Later on the way home, I determined that I could hide the Shyster from my mom by depositing it under my bed. Many of my peers had begun hiding "girly magazines" under their beds; my equally sinful secret was to conceal fishing lures.

Being two years older than I was, Rick had limited time to spend with a 14-year-old like me. But I had witnessed how much a vehicle could increase one's chances for angling success, and I knew whose wheels could help me achieve it—my Granddaddy Willie's.

Growing up, I had two role models: North Carolina Coach Dean Smith, who has greatly influenced the way I teach high school students, and Granddaddy Willie. The latter did not care anything about fishing, but he also did not approve of how his son, my father, would rail against it and refuse to take me.

So that summer, Granddaddy and I planned an epic, secret excursion to the New River. Granddaddy kindly gave me some money which I used to buy a lure that even Rick did not possess—a Rebel Minnow, a classic hard plastic stickbait. On the day of our adventure, Granddaddy picked me up and told my parents that we were "going riding" (an extremely honest man, he would never have lied to my parents, but he understood the wisdom of concealing the truth), and drove us to the New, said he would watch me from the shore, and told me to go wade fishing and have fun.

All those formative years of wading Gish's Branch served me well that day on the New, as I already knew how to slowly and softly drag my feet across the substrate, so as not to disturb the multitude of creatures that lived there or create the ripples that would alarm any nearby smallmouths. For three hours within sight of my Grandfather, I waded the New, employing the Rebel to catch two fine smallmouths, an honest seven-incher and one slightly smaller. In my angling soul, I now felt that I truly could refer to myself as "a bass fisherman."

When I became old enough to begin the process of earning a driver's license, I did so initially not to date girls but to broaden my fishing horizons. My dad ran a small used car lot from our house, so when I gained a license he allowed me to drive what he proclaimed was the worst car on the lot, a shabby looking, red 1962 Chevy Malibu convertible that featured gashes in its rollback canopy, signs of multiple fender benders, and a missing hubcap for the left rear tire.

Dad knew I was using the car for fishing, I knew he knew, but we never spoke of the other's knowledge, so a sort of uneasy truce developed between us. But he did assert his parental authority after one ill-begotten trout fishing trip where I drove a then unheard of distance of 30 miles from home.

Two buddies and I had decided to spend an April Saturday at a trout stream and we determined that to beat the crowds we would arise well before sunrise and begin the long trek. On the way there, part of the Malibu's decaying canopy peeled off in the dark and landed who knows where. Soon after we arrived, one of my cohorts fell in the creek, I did the same later, and the result was that upon my arriving home, Dad found a car with part of its roof missing, wet car seats, and muddy floor boards. He sold the Malibu within a week and in its place gave me a car he called "Goldfinger."

Goldfinger, so named in part because it was a yellow 1963 Ford, had a broken gas gauge and gobbled fuel like no other vehicle I have ever driven. It was also named Goldfinger because Dad had jokingly remarked that only the James Bond character could afford to drive the Ford with its extravagant gas consumption.

Never knowing how much gas Goldfinger possessed in its tank and knowing whatever there was inside would soon be expended, I was constantly stopping at filling stations to replenish the supply and even then the car frequently ran out of petrol while I was on my fishing trips. Thus Dad had once again hampered my wanderlust without ever saying a word.

Years more passed and I graduated from college, found a place to live, and eventually became infatuated with a woman who stirred my soul even more than smallmouths did—no small feat. For our third date, I asked Elaine to go smallmouth fishing with me. She said yes and later, she answered again in the affirmative when I asked her to marry me.

Now much has changed in my life. Besides becoming a teacher, I also became an outdoor writer, proving my father incorrect when he said I would never make any money from fishing. Mom even became quite proud of my writing, subscribing to magazines if they ran her son's stories and purchasing my books on river smallmouth fishing to give to friends.

Elaine and I have two wonderful children, and Sarah and Mark enjoy fishing although they are not as fanatical as I am about this most marvelous pastime. We even live on a rural property that a smallie stream flows through and own another parcel that features a headwater spring of the New River. And today at 64, when I go fishing it is almost always to streams where I quest after smallmouths and trout. Because for me, the fascination began at five.

The Day I Became a Deer Hunter

On the morning of November 21, 1988, opening day of Virginia's general firearms season, I awoke, determined that by the end of this day if someone were to ask me if I were a deer hunter, I could honestly answer yes. It was not as if I had never gone deer hunting. I had...for three long, frustrating years.

And it was true that I had actually tagged a whitetail, but the kill was a fraud and I knew it. Coming from a non-hunting, non-fishing family, I had never had anyone to mentor me about the outdoors. Finally, as a 33-year-old in 1985, I asked my father-in-law Ernie Adams if I could tag along on one of his hunt club's treks into the Virginia mountains.

Mr. Adams kindly agreed and arranged for me to be one of the standers during the day's many deer drives. To make sure that I did nothing foolish, especially taking a risky or potentially dangerous shot, my father-in-law set up within a few yards of me. When a 4-pointer scudded by some 30 yards distant and 20 minutes into the initial drive of the day, I fired and seconds later, so did Mr. Adams.

Even as a novice, I knew that I had blown the shot, but Mr. Adams generously proclaimed that it was he who had missed and that I had just killed my first whitetail. Feeling guilty about my father-in-law's act of kindness and ashamed at my lack of prowess with a gun, my despair reached its nadir when I learned that the deer had apparently been wounded days before and gangrene had set in. The meat was not fit to eat.

Although I went afield with Mr. Adams' hunt club several more times during the 1985 season, I never felt comfortable doing so. I knew virtually nothing about how to pursue whitetails, but I became absolutely, and obsessively, sure about two things—I wanted to take on deer one-on-one, alone in the woods with only my woodsmanship, such as it was, to guide me. If I failed to figure out this creature's travel patterns, foods, bedding areas, or any other nuance, no one but me would be to blame.

But if I were to successfully figure out what the deer were doing and a kill occurred, I could experience a type of satisfaction that must be profound for all those individuals who had accomplished what, at this point in my life, surely must be a miraculous feat. I could revel in the thrill of the chase and its successful conclusion as humans have been doing for millennia.

And second, and just as intensely, I wanted to own and live on land where I could hunt deer. As public school teachers and with two children under the age of seven, my wife Elaine and I were perpetually short of money, especially since we were putting aside money for Sarah and Mark's college educations. I knew I would have to find a second job in order to buy the land.

As an English teacher, I had always loved writing and teaching my students how to be more accomplished at this skill. So I enrolled in a writing class at a local college. The the first night I almost dropped out.

The professor asked each student to introduce himself or herself and explain why we wanted to be writers; I soon realized I had come to the wrong place. The first responder said she wanted to write poetry that would make the world weep; the second said he wanted to pen the next great American novel, the third proclaimed that she wanted to compose essays that would change the way people thought. When my turn came...

"I need a second job, so I can buy land out in the country that I can deer hunt on."

The poet smirked, the novelist moaned, the essayist shuddered, and the professor displayed a pained expression and quickly moved on to the next student.

For our first assignment, the professor, who had never actually published anything, but was working on numerous book, short story, and poetry projects, told us to write something that we thought could be sent to a publisher. We had a week to write the rough draft and a month to complete the assignment.

I knew that I didn't have enough knowledge to scribble something on deer hunting, so I wrote a story about how to fish creeks. When the class work shopped my article the next meeting, the professor humiliated me by stating that I had misunderstood the assignment, that no one would purchase that type of thing. He further told me to forget about that particular story and to write something else for the next class.

Embarrassed and enraged, I said nothing but the next morning I mailed the story to *Virginia Wildlife* and a few days later the editor wrote back stating that she was buying the story, a check soon would be in the mail, and would I please consider sending another story to her.

Beaming, I read the letter to the class at the next meeting and presented the rough draft of my next outdoors story. The professor, though, was not amused, stating once again that I had not followed directions. When the class mercifully ended two months later, every student received an *A* except for one... it's not hard to guess who that was.

But I was now a professional outdoor writer and every morning I awoke early before school to write and every week I sent a story away to the outdoor magazines. As the checks came in, Elaine and I deposited them in our "deer land account," which was sacred and inviolate—money could not be withdraw from it unless it was to buy writing supplies, or on some future glorious day, the rural property itself.

Like penny pinching misers, Elaine and I hoarded my writing money and in 1988, we purchased 29 acres at the terminus of a dead end road in Botetourt County, Virginia. For me the decision to buy the land was clinched when I found deer droppings (I had developed enough woodsmanship to identify them) while the real estate agent showed us the property.

So before dawn on that long ago November 21 morning, I walked to the edge of a pine glade that marks the end of the property. And not long after dawn broke, I glimpsed a spike walking by 25 yards away. Trembling, I mounted the Remington 700 bolt action and shot… and missed. Shaking worse, I shot again…and missed again. The little buck, as dumb as I was inexperienced, stood staring at me. I shot once more and this time the buck fell.

Having never considered the fact that I might need a drag rope, I spent over an hour hauling the spike (by his tiny antlers) the 150 yards back to the house. The trek was made more arduous because I had no idea how to field dress a whitetail. (I had left the instructions on how to do so, torn from an *Outdoor Life* magazine, at home.)

The exhausting drag, the ensuing confusion once I reached home about how to gut a deer, the bleeding cut on my left index finger which occurred during the field dressing… none of that mattered. For that third shot had made one thing absolutely certain—at last I could call myself a deer hunter.

I have two closing thoughts for my fellow QDMA members. Our organization rightfully places a great deal of emphasis on mentoring kids, new hunters, and adults about the outdoor world and whitetails. If you have the chance to mentor someone this year, please take advantage of the opportunity. The folks you help will very likely one day want to join us.

And, second, another admirable part of the QDMA philosophy is that it is perfectly all right for kids and novices to kill a yearling or any non-trophy buck. As these individuals new to the pastime progress in their knowledge and skills, the time will likely come when they will only want to take a mature buck. But for now any buck, doe, or yearling should be considered a trophy as that spike was for me that long ago November morning.

Hunting the Living Meat

"I want you to do the next step by yourself," I say to my friend Doak who has just killed his second-ever deer. With my encouragement three years earlier, Doak took up the pastime of deer hunting, attending a hunting education class, going on scouting expeditions, purchasing hunting clothing, learning about whitetail foods, and finally going hunting.

When Doak killed his first deer, I did all the field dressing, slowly explaining the steps needed to remove the viscera and avoid contaminating any of the meat. Understandably, it was overwhelming to him, as it would be to anyone who has just seen the body cavity of a creature opened (especially an animal that the individual has killed) and viewed a confusing array of organs, blood, and muscles.

After Doak shot his second whitetail, I asked him if he would like to begin the field dressing process by himself, but the uncertainty showing in his eyes followed by the request that the act be done just one more time by me led me to make the initial cut into the body cavity. I continue the field dressing process until all that is left is the severing of the windpipe and esophagus.

As I grapple with how to explain to Doak how he is to reach deep inside the deer's cavity to sever the "cord" which will, in turn, lead to him pulling out the viscera, thus completing the most primitive part of the field dressing, I think of a quote that sometimes comes to mind after I have killed a deer.

The phrase is Jack London's "hunting their living meat" from *Call of the Wild*. In my English 9 class at the high school where I teach, London's story of the dog Buck's metamorphosis into a wolf is part of my syllabus. This epic's lyrical prose sings to me as a hunter, and I hope and believe as well to my students as human beings.

The specific phrase "hunting their living meat" comes near the end of the novel when the author compares the carnivorous nature of the Yeehats (a fictional Indian tribe in the book) to that of a wolf pack that Buck seems destined to join. We hunters certainly don't live as close to the primeval state as wolves or Native Americans when we make a kill, even if the animal has been killed with a bow.

But we come somewhat close to the primordial soup of life when we field dress a whitetail and nearer still when we butcher the animal and then eat what was the "living meat." How can I communicate to Doak the necessity, the special nature, the awe of reaching into the deer's cavity and severing the windpipe and gullet?

"Would you cut the windpipe for me just like you did with the first deer?" asks Doak.

"No, I want you to do it," I reply. "I might not be with you when you kill your next deer. Put on your gutting gloves and reach deep inside the upper chest."

Doak dons his gloves and tentatively begins to feel around the cavity.

"I think I've found the cord," he says. "Do I just cut right through it?"

"Yes, but cut slowly, you don't want to cut yourself. I've cut myself several times when I've gotten in a hurry."

Blanching just a little, Doak slices through the windpipe and esophagus and inquires what to do next.

"Use the cord to gently pull the entire pile out, you're almost done."

My friend pulls the entire mass out and clear of the animal. Doak sports a huge grin.

"I did it," he beams.

"Great job, next time you can do the whole field dressing thing by yourself."

I look at my friend, and he is suddenly shaking, a delayed reaction to the enormity of the actions he has just experienced — the killing of a creature and helping with its disemboweling. My thoughts once again turn to a quote from *Call of the Wild*.

"There is an ecstasy that marks the summit of life, and beyond which life cannot rise. And such is the paradox of living, this ecstasy comes when one is most alive, and it comes as a complete forgetfulness that one is alive."

Doak is experiencing that ecstasy.

"I'm sorry, I don't know what's come over me, I'm so happy but I'm shaking all over...it's the adrenaline, I guess," he says.

"I understand. It's normal, it's natural, it's okay, don't feel ashamed," I say.

Then I remember my most recent bout with deer fever and begin to tell the story to reassure my friend that the reaction to what he has just accomplished is not unusual.

"A couple of Octobers ago, I was bow-hunting over at the Alderson place; you know the woodlot that borders the pasture?" I begin. "These two fawns come slowly walking toward my tree stand. The wind is right, the two fawns haven't a clue I'm there, and I decide to take the doe yearling with my compound.

"I try to draw back, and I start to hyperventilate so bad that it's like my arms are paralyzed. I'm shaking and breathing hard. I'm an absolute mess."

"That's awful, did you blow the shot?"

"Well, by this time the fawns are just 10 yards away, and I still haven't got myself together. Then I start fussing at myself to calm down, take a few deep breaths, and remind myself that this isn't the first time I've been in this situation.

"All of a sudden I stop hyperventilating, I get my nerves together, draw back, and send an arrow right through the fawn. It goes only about 15 yards and collapses—a quick, clean merciful kill, just what you want to happen."

"That's amazing, I bet you've killed way over a hundred deer."

"Yeah, but I guarantee that I will hyperventilate again, who knows when, either this year, next, or some season soon. And that's not the worst of it."

"What do you mean?"

"I can't fall asleep until sometime after midnight every time I kill a deer. I keep replaying in mind over and over the hunt, the deer approaching, the shot, the climbing down from the tree stand, finding and following the blood trail—finding the deer and the overwhelming joy of finding that deer that comes afterwards. It's so intense.

"It's like that line from *Call of the Wild*, 'hunting the living meat.' I don't think the size of the deer has anything to do with the way my body reacts. The whole thing is just so close to the raw essence of being alive."

No words are spoken for a while, and the field where Doak killed the deer has now grown quite dark. Then I say.

"Now, I've got a question for you. Just out of curiosity, how did you sleep the night after you killed your first deer?"

"Just awful, I kept tossing and turning. I was still too charged up, even hours after the hunt."

"Here's to more sleepless nights for you. Give me your gun and daypack. I'll carry them. But I want you to drag your deer out, that's part of the experience, too. When we get back to the car, you can phone check your deer, then we'll drive to my butcher's.

"Maybe the next deer you kill, you and I can butcher it. That's something worth experiencing, too."

And I could have added—should have added—that's it all part of the lifestyle of hunting the living meat.

It's My Dirt

"It's my dirt! Eh-heh! No good, but it's—it's mine, all mine." So says Grandpa Joad in the classic 1940 movie about the Great Depression, *The Grapes of Wrath*. As a high school English teacher in Botetourt County, Virginia, I teach this epic work to my tenth graders. And every year when I come to this powerful scene where Grandpa Joad (who has just suffered the humiliation of having his family and himself evicted from the land they have farmed for generations) proclaims his innermost thoughts, I pause the film and ask the students if any one of them understands the special nature and obligation of owning land. I also inquire if any one of them has the dream of owning rural land that they can be stewards of and be a part of.

I believe these are universal questions worth asking of any American, of any age, of any time period. I also believe that QDMA members, more than many if not most sportsmen, understand the symbiotic relationship between man and soil, to the sublime benefit of both. For it is the soil, as Grandpa Joad well knew, that gives nourishment to all we hope to achieve as landowners, sportsmen, and stewards of the wild world.

So how do my students answer these questions? Often, understandably, they are confused, for, as is true with most of the country, these young folks dwell in suburbia. But, often, I also have a few students who live in the country, and they then raise their hands and talk about how much having land to live on means to them, and how one day they would "like to have a place."

It is then, as these young folks are now rapt with an eagerness to learn more, that I launch into what it means to be a part of the land. I tell them that on the 38 acres that my wife Elaine and I live on, we try to be in touch (both on a figurative and literal level) with the life-nourishing soil throughout the year. In the spring, we'll root out invasive species like sericea lespedeza and ailanthus that threaten native vegetation and we'll plant a garden as well. And always there's a patch of open ground that will be ideal for a stand of little bluestem or some other native warm season grass or a plant or tree or maybe even a small food plot.

I will also tell the students of the otherworldly joy that exists come spring when I hear the thundering pronouncements of a mature gobbler behind the house, how I will run toward him, stop and set up some 75 yards away and then begin to imitate the sounds of a turkey hen. The girls will laugh and the boys smirk when I tell them that the tom thinks that the originator of those sounds is a creature that he wants to mate with.

Come summer, we'll reap the benefits of the healthy soil as we gather vegetables and pick wild blackberries, raspberries, and dewberries from the young forest we created behind the house when we harvested some diseased pines. We'll dine on redbreast sunfish and rock bass that thrive in the creek that runs through our property; a stream that features a robust riparian zone that we have allowed to lushly grow up.

We'll watch fledgling bluebirds emerge from the boxes that we have positioned, and pileated and downy woodpeckers do the same from the dead trees we have left standing. And we'll awake early in the morning to listen to the lyrical notes of whip-poor-wills, the unnerving quavering of screech owls, and the haunting reverberations of great horned owls. By the time I let the chickens out of their henhouse, it is time for the best radio station in the world to sign on — the one that plays the music of cardinals, towhees, and Carolina wrens as they greet first light.

In the fall, the heat from the trees we harvest will keep us warm, and the oaks, hickories, dogwoods, and cherries (from which around those other trees were cut) will bear more mast to help keep the wildlife alive through the winter to come. And some of the deer and turkeys that live on our land will provide us with nourishment as well.

I will also tell my young charges that nothing in the outdoors makes me feel more alive and in tune with the earth than arrowing an October whitetail deer, following a blood trail through the forest, and periodically dropping to my knees and intensely studying the leaf litter for the faintest fleck of the life giving blood. And I will relate that nothing in the outdoors makes me feel more reverent and more joyful than when I come across the deer whose life I have just taken and whose meat will bring life giving nourishment to Elaine and me. I will confess that I often will gently and lovingly pat a flank of the deer and my eyes grow misty for a moment before I begin the field dressing process.

Come winter, I will explain how Elaine and I will walk our land and make plans for its future, as given the open nature of the woods in winter, no other season is better for ascertaining what needs to be done to make the soil more life sustaining. I'll also level a few red cedars so that the songbirds, mammals, and other creatures have more horizontal cover to survive those long winter nights. And on those rare, warm, late winter afternoons, we will study the soil in order to try to fathom if it is ready to emerge from its long slumber.

I know that Elaine and I are but temporary owners of our land and soil, but we want to be good stewards during the ephemeral moment in time we are part of it, the proverbial "working on it" as *The Grapes of Wrath* character Muley Graves proclaims. "That's what make it our'n, bein' born on it… and workin' on it… and and dying' on it! And not no piece of paper with the writin' on it!"

As people who know and care about the importance of the soil, we QDMAers well understand Muley's sentiments—sentiments that we should endeavor to uphold and share with others so that they too (like hopefully my students now do) will know that the soil is the essence of life.

She Still Can't Cast

A story of true love and trout fishing

"Hi, my name is Elaine. What's yours?" At our first meeting in the summer of 1974, with her words spoken in the decidedly unromantic setting of a summer-camp laundry room, Elaine Adams cast a spell on me. But I soon learned she was that friendly to everyone and had no special interest in me.

She was the sweetest, prettiest girl I had ever met, with bewitching green eyes under long eyelashes, and from our laundry room encounter onward, I had a desperate, hopeless crush on her. Many times during the two summers we worked together at the camp, I plotted just how to ask her out, but the timing never seemed right, mostly because she had a long line of suitors. I silently raged every time I saw her with any of them.

The closest I came to actually inquiring about a date was at the start of our second summer at camp. I had some interest in a girl named Sue, a counselor in the same cabin where Elaine worked, so my scheme was to ask both girls after supper if they wanted to go canoeing with me on a creek that flowed through the camp. My hope was that Elaine would show some interest (highly unlikely) and if not, perhaps Sue would flirt and I could ask her out instead.

Predictably, during the entire time I paddled the two ladies about, Elaine was largely silent while Sue joked and laughed. Encouraged by the latter's actions, I asked Sue out, and she and I dated a few times that summer. But I couldn't stop thinking about Elaine—a condition that persisted the rest of the summer of 1975.

Two years later, camp administrators announced a reunion, and I called the organizers to see who was on the list of attendees. Elaine wasn't among them, so I gave the organizers Elaine's number and suggested that they call her. When she strolled into the reunion that spring day, I immediately walked over to her, noted her bare ring finger, and decided to ask her for a date. Still intimidated by this gorgeous female, I hesitated for three hours until the reunion was about to end. After I asked her out, she started flipping through her date book.

"I can't this weekend, I have dates Friday and Saturday."

"How about the next weekend?"

More flipping: "I'm booked that Friday and Saturday, too."

Determined right then and there to either attain a date with her or to be permanently and humiliatingly rejected, I slogged onward. "How about three weekends from now?"

More flipping, and then: "I can't that Friday, but I am free on Saturday."

On our first date, we went out to dinner; the second, bowling; and afterwards we stayed up until 2:00 A.M. talking about anything and everything.

For our third date, I asked her to go on a combination fishing and camping trip on a property where I had permission to go afield. I figured she should find out early in our relationship how much the outdoors meant to me. After toting the camping gear to the creek bank, I offered to take Elaine on her maiden fishing trip. And I thought it might be gallant for me to show her how to cast and hopefully hook and land a fish.

Thinking that it would be easier to teach her how to use a spinning rod than a fly rod, I started her out with the former. However, the casting tutorial could not have gone worse. On her first cast, Elaine hurled one of my favorite lures into an unforgiving sycamore. Overcompensating for losing one lure to a tree, she flung the next bait into the water at our feet. The third cast resulted in a crankbait spiraling high into the air and landing four feet from our position. On the fourth cast, she threw the crankbait into a logjam.

In one sense I was dismayed that she refused to make a fifth cast, yet secretly glad as the cost in lures was mounting. Elaine was an apathetic angler. But no matter, the sheer joy I experienced when I positioned her arms and hands to show her proper casting motions made my heart ache.

That evening, we cuddled around the campfire until the embers faded. Our outing ended prematurely after midnight when Elaine experienced a migraine headache and asked if I would take her home. When we arrived there, she told me how sweet I had been to see to her needs first, knowing how much I loved fishing.

On our fourth date, we went to see *Rocky*, and afterwards, when we arrived at my house, she said, "You know I love you."

"I love you, too. Want to go shopping for rings tomorrow?"

"Yes," she said.

It wasn't much of a proposal, I guess, but I did buy her an engagement ring the next day, and we were married the following June. After the honeymoon and settling into our home, I still had an unresolved matter with her—to teach her how to cast and enjoy fishing, daring to hope that she might even try fly fishing.

On one of our early river excursions, we went with a guide who, after watching Elaine continuously make her infamous four-foot long casts, chivalrously took on my wife as his personal project. The man's tutorial did not go well as she chucked cast after cast high into the streamside greenery. Finally, the guide could take no more.

"Little darling," the Southern gentleman drawled. "It's a little-known fact that sometimes the fish crawl out of the water and climb onto the limbs of trees and sun themselves with the squirrels. You just keep on casting up there, and sooner or later you'll catch one of them type fish."

Elaine Ingram with a wild brown trout caught from a mountain stream.

Then there was our trip to the New River. I had called the guide in advance to tell him that my spouse was not a "particularly good caster and doesn't seem to take well to instruction." His solution was to tie a Heddon Tiny Torpedo to Elaine's line, position my wife in the back of his drift boat, and tell her to just let her lure float with the current. He and I would concentrate on catching smallmouths so that I could photograph them for a story assignment.

His plan was brilliant on multiple levels, but the strangest thing happened. It was one of those uncommon days when the smallies wanted their prey drifted aimlessly in the current. Bronzeback after bronzeback rose up to smash the Torpedo, and by the time we broke for shore lunch, Elaine had caught an astounding 13 fish while the guide and I didn't have a half dozen between us.

The guide praised Elaine's fishing abilities to the heavens, and went off to prepare our meal. It was then that she spoke words that made me fear that she would never desire to be an angler.

"Would you take that blame Torpedo thing off my line," she demanded. "The fish won't leave it alone. I can't get any reading done."

After that trip, our joint fishing endeavors evolved into my going fishing and her reading a book in the stern of our canoe. Maybe the fates hadn't meant for her to share my angling passion, and as was true from the first time I met her, I was overjoyed just to be in her company.

Thirty wonderful years passed with the most perfect wife imaginable, except for that little fishing flaw. Then two events happened in the fall of 2008. First, a magazine assigned me to do a story on Casting for Recovery (a national organization that offers retreats for women with or recovering from breast cancer, combining fly fishing, counseling, and medical expertise.) And secondly, ironically—Elaine was diagnosed with a virulent strain of breast cancer.

All through two rounds of chemotherapy and the mastectomy, we kept focusing on a goal for her—that she would recover enough to go with me to the 2009 CFR retreat in North Carolina, where we would act as press observers and she would help me with the interviews for the story.

The Sunday we spent at the retreat was an emotional one for us, as we interviewed numerous women who had survived breast cancer and found fly fishing a superlative way to help them focus on their own recoveries.

On the way home, Elaine said, "I think I would like to go to a Casting for Recovery retreat next year."

"Well, sweetheart, you know you would have to go fly fishing with the other ladies," I haltingly replied.

"Maybe the fly fishing part wouldn't be too bad," she said. "After all, they have guides who help you with the casting."

Elaine was chosen as one of the participants for the 2010 CFR retreat, and she came back a changed woman.

"I caught two trout on flies," she bubbled as she came through the door. "I learned how to cast. I made my own flies. You want to go trout fishing this weekend?"

Indeed, she had experienced a transformation, and we began to go fly fishing together. Now Elaine truly enjoys tying flies at the vise I gave her for

Christmas in 2010. This past Christmas, she gave me the most magnificent present I have ever received—a fly tied from a turkey feather that came from a bird I had called in and killed.

Come this next June, we will have been married for 38 years, and we now own the land where we first went fishing in 1977. Elaine has her own fly rod and fishes exclusively with it. However, despite the tutoring she received at the CFR retreat, Elaine still can't cast. And you know what? It still doesn't matter to me.

ALSO BY BRUCE INGRAM

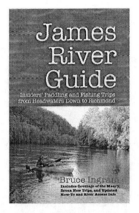

The James River is Virginia's premier river for recreation, and the *James River Guide* is the key to enjoying it, whether you are an angler, kayaker, rafter, or bird watcher. Twenty-nine locator maps provide vital information on the river, all the way from its headwaters near Iron Gate to the dramatic fall line at Richmond.

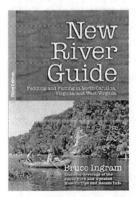

The New River is one of the most changeable and fickle rivers on the East Coast—and also one of the most beautiful and rewarding. It attracts anglers, canoeists, kayakers, rafters, bird watchers, rock climbers, and those who simply enjoy the great outdoors. The *New River Guide* provides an indispensable overview of this untamed and scenic waterway as it winds through three states, including the bucolic South Fork in North Carolina, the ridges of Virginia, and the gorges of West Virginia.

Fly and Spin Fishing for River Smallmouths is a motivating, informative guide for nature lovers of all kinds. The book delves into river bass fishing with easy-to-use tips on everything smallmouth, from lures and flies, types of cover to target, to strategies for cold and warm seasons, and much more. The book suggests thrilling family-friendly river hobbies like canoeing, bird watching, river camping, and introducing children to the outdoors.